Reclaiming Intimacy

IN YOUR MARRIAGE

Reclaiming Intimacy

IN YOUR MARRIAGE

Robert & Debra Bruce

BETHANY HOUSE PUBLISHERS
MINNEAPOLIS, MINNESOTA 55438

Published by Bethany House Publishers
A Ministry of Bethany Fellowship, Inc.
11300 Hampshire Avenue South
Minneapolis, Minnesota 55438

Printed in the United States of America.

Library of Congress Cataloging-in-Publication Data

Bruce, Robert G., 1949–
    Reclaiming intimacy in your marriage / Robert & Debra Bruce.
      p.   cm.
    ISBN 1–55661–807–7 (pbk.).
    ISBN 1–55661–907–3 (lg. print)
    1. Marriage—United States. 2. Marriage—Religious aspects—
Christianity. 3. Married people—Religious life—United States.
4. Intimacy (Psychology). I. Bruce, Debra Fulghum, 1951–   II. Title.
HQ536.B775   1996
306.81—dc20   96–25293
                                               CIP

ROBERT AND DEBRA BRUCE, after twenty-three years of marriage, are still best friends. Robert is the Senior Pastor of Ortega United Methodist Church in Jacksonville, Florida. Debra is a full-time writer with more than 2,400 articles and twenty-two books to her credit in both the ABA and CBA markets. The Bruces have three children and live in Florida.

Contents

INTRODUCTION

You CAN Reclaim Intimacy in Your Marriage

When couples come to us and say, "You probably won't understand what we are going through, but we don't even know each other anymore," we affirm their confession. We have also experienced times in our twenty-three-year marriage where too many commitments and excessive giving to others consumed any chance of alone or intimate time together.

About twelve years ago, Robert's busy career as senior pastor of a large church and his leadership involvement on church and community committees, as well as numerous speaking commitments, kept him going in overdrive from dawn to late hours at night. Evenings were filled with board meetings, committees, and volunteer groups. In the midst of all this, he made time to coach three Little League teams—T-ball, softball, and baseball—one for each of our children. Deb's freelance writing put her in overload as she got up well before 5:00 A.M. each morning to spend long days—six days a week—working on book proposals, assignments, and tight deadlines, while teaching the young adult Sunday school class, directing the children's choir, car-pooling kids to lessons each day, and serving as president of the middle school's Parent-Teacher Organization. In the midst of our work and nighttime volunteering were three very energetic and challenging children—Rob, Brittnye, and Ashley—who required attention from Mom and Dad, as well as help with homework and peer problems.

To be honest, twelve years ago we simply resigned ourselves to the fact that this schedule was our "way of life." After all, our friends told of being stressed-out too . . . until one day when Bob was diagnosed with a benign and treatable heart condition that his doctor said could be life-threatening IF he did not slow down.

That was the moment we discovered the reality of how God can speak to you through life's unexpected interruptions. Somehow, while sitting together in the cardiac ward of the hospital with Bob hooked up to all sorts of machines that monitored his irregular and racing heart rate, all of the proposals, Little League teams, committees, sermons, and presentations did not matter. All that was really important was holding on to our precious relationship and leaning on God's promise of strength and abiding love as we reset our goals and priorities— as a couple and a team.

We had a wake-up call early in our marriage while we were still young enough to reassess our relationship and make much-needed changes to reclaim intimacy. But what about those relationships where marital partners avoid intimacy or emotional and physical closeness? Some say it is normal for a marriage relationship to get "comfortable" as partners become preoccupied with kids, careers, and personal interests. But we contend that the longer a marriage goes feeling too comfortable— without intimacy—the more difficult it is to pull it off the back burner when adversity hits, when you need to face trials . . . together.

Divorce rates have been on a roller coaster in this country since the end of World War I, when family life was fairly stable and the divorce rates were low. Since the end of World War II, divorce rates have steadily increased—from about 10 percent in the early 1950s to a rate that approaches 50 percent today. As a country, the United States has the highest divorce rate in the world.[1]

Start Your Intimate Journey

We believe that divorce can be a decision of the past and feel that *almost every relationship* is salvageable. As you begin the Intimate Journey outlined in this book, we must tell you that the next eight challenges you undertake will *really work* to strengthen the weaknesses in your marriage and cement the emotional bonds between you and your spouse. And we speak from personal experience when we say that reclaiming intimacy in your marriage is more important than any other thing in life, except for your personal relationship with Jesus Christ. Since our personal awakening twelve years ago, we have realized that the unending obstacles we face in life with busy careers, constant chores, rambunctious kids, and continual commitments will never go away . . . but they can be managed. We have discovered some workable, positive measures in how to control and cope with these marriage zappers so that our energy and time can be spent on strengthening the emotional connectedness in our marriage. Then when life's interruptions hit, we are able to face these . . . together.

In our marriage, we strive to complete each other. Bob is quiet, contemplative, and a thinker; Debra is extroverted, responsive, and a doer. Not only do we complement each other, we also give each other security. We have found that in an intimate marriage, we are the very best of friends, filling in those missing links in the other's life and looking forward to growing old together as we enjoy the emotional side of love.

But what is this emotional side of love? And what does this mean to those of us today who feel as if we are in constant overdrive twenty-four hours a day . . . even as we sleep—IF we sleep? Let's be honest. Do we really have time for intimacy in marriage today?

Intimacy, both emotional and physical, means personal closeness and openness. In our twenty-three-year marriage, we have found intimacy to be that passionate state where we can reveal our inner selves without fear of rejection. Intimacy gives us strength, affirmation, and support in our relationship, and because we feel secure it sets us free to be distinct individuals. We can be "who we are" in marriage as we become emotionally intimate.

Contrary to the beliefs of many, intimacy is not just a mere psychological fad or a rallying cry of couples in the nineties. Intimacy is based on a deep biological need.[2] And from our experience of counseling couples in this decade, we find the need for intimacy is growing; people need emotional involvement with others to face the multiple challenges life presents.

Perhaps one reason for this growing need for intimate relationships is due to our transient society. In years past, people lived close to family members and relied on parents and siblings for affirmation, empathy, emotional strength, even after marriage. When suffering occurred, people could turn to relatives for comfort and support to help bear the pain. But with our highly mobile society, many married couples today are as we are—living hundreds of miles away from parents and siblings. This situation mandates that our marriage be intimately bonded, for when bad things happen in our lives, we have no one to talk to but each other.

If you're like most people today, you are overwhelmed by the frantic pace of life. Perhaps you admit to being caught up in the whirlwind of daily living with runaway schedules, careers that take precedence over personal and family needs, unruly children, rebellious teens, nightly fast food, no time to exercise, and no time for self.

The problem with living such an overly committed life filled with careers, commitments, and chaos is that in the midst of the harried and often meaningless days, our emotional needs are ignored. While you may intellectually understand that both an orderly life and a sense of direction are vital to your overall well-being, the demands you face each day make either one difficult to attain. It is quite easy to be trapped by the demands of our secular world and to forget our intimate and spiritual needs.

Intimacy Is Not for Women Only

You may have thought that women are more prone to seek intimacy in marriage, but we have had many men tell us of feeling empty and alone instead of emotionally connected with their wife. One recent study found that in a test group of 1,049 men and women aged eighteen to sixty-five, nearly eight out of ten respondents said it is difficult to have sex without emotional involvement. While most women have traditionally linked sex with emotional involvement, more men are now agreeing. In 1984, 59 percent of men studied said they found it difficult to have sex without emotional involvement. A staggering 71 percent of men studied in America today said that the emotional side of sex was very important. In both studies, 86 percent of women said they felt this way.[3]

Intimacy Is More Than Sex

Now for those who associate intimacy with sex and assume that the next eight challenges are about perfecting an intimate sexual relationship within marriage, we must let you know that they are not. We will refer you to books written by professionals for this aspect of intimacy. But we will discuss how through our experiences and the advice given to us by others, your sexual relationship and every other part of your life will be greatly enhanced as you are intimately and emotionally connected. You and your partner can begin to reclaim the passion and yearning you once had for each other if you make this your priority. You see, we believe that without intimacy in a marriage, "making love" is merely "having sex." And there is a world of emotional and spiritual difference between the two!

Life's Interruptions Will Hit

Why is reclaiming intimacy so important to couples today? Through our experiences, we have found there is a common link that unifies all people, and millions of people are just starting to feel its tug. At some point, we will all face the illness of a loved one—perhaps even terminal illness and death. Many of us will have to move. More likely than not, we will change jobs at some time, and we may even lose a job. And every person we talk to tells of having more month than money, problems raising kids and teens, stresses coping with aging or ill parents, and almost daily feelings of being overwhelmed, overworked, and overloaded. Many couples are wanting more from life, and more from their marriages, and are beginning to look for a way off of this endless treadmill.

The problem, as we see it, is that we have become a hurried generation, taking very little time to sit down with our family for a meal, visit with in-laws and friends, hug our children, listen to our spouses, know our neighbors . . . or even pray.

What about your life? Have you put your marriage, your intimate partnership, first? Isn't there always just one more deadline to meet, project to finish, phone call or appointment to make, errand to run, face to wipe, or client to see? Perhaps this is why when life's interruptions and afflictions unexpectedly hit (and they do hit—they are not planned!), most of us have no inner strength or coping skills in our marital relationship to deal with these—unless we are intimately bonded with our spouse.

We know personally that life's interruptions affect every part of our being. But we have also experienced that the more emotionally linked we are, the more equipped we are as the Bruce team to stand united against adversities. And we have seen that in marriage, just as in sports, the strongest team survives the opposition and ultimately comes out ahead!

Intimacy Is All About Taking Risks

As you read this book, we are going to ask you to do some real soul-searching and risk taking, for taking risks is a major part of an intimate relationship. The willingness to let down your guard and to share yourself, the good and the bad, with another is not easy! But to fully bond with your spouse as you strengthen your marriage, you must give up all fear of rejection or abandonment and share the emotional levels of your life from the lowest ebbs of sadness, fears, and depression to the exhilarating highs of happiness, hopes, and dreams. And, as most married couples know, these emotional ups and downs or interruptions in a marriage do not just happen at will . . . but they do happen.

Recently we were awakened around 3:30 A.M. with a phone call. Deb's sister Lori was thrilled. "My contractions started, and I'm in labor. Can you come now to take care of JoJo [her son] so I can get to the hospital?" She had just spoken those joyous words of celebration when the phone beeped with call waiting. Two calls at exactly 3:30 A.M.?

"Bob," a church member cried. "My husband just died. Can you come now to help us?"

Two phone calls in a fifteen-second span of time: one full of joy and hope; one filled with shock and personal sorrow. In that brief moment of our marriage, we experienced two life interruptions: the emotional high of celebrating new life and the untimely sadness and loss of a close friend and church member.

And such is life. The emotional levels or hills and valleys within a relationship are never planned. Intimacy means that we take the risk of expressing our deepest emotions with our spouse, both the joy and the pain. When we are intimately bonded in this way, instead of being sidetracked by never-ending demands on our time and energies, we are better equipped to handle life's interruptions. We can cope with crises by leaning on the strength found in our personal relationship with Jesus Christ and our abiding love for each other.

Intimacy Will Enhance Your Entire Life

Intimacy affects every part of life—our self-esteem, our friendships, our family relationships, our career motivation, and more. When you are intimately involved with your spouse, you feel energized and have enthusiasm for life. When you feel loved and understood by your spouse, your relationships with others deepen, and you have a sense of fulfillment. And when you are intimately connected, you can face adversity head on, knowing that you can lean on each other and on your faith in Jesus Christ.

As we have shared, all of us will face interruptions in our lives, some more painful than others. But one thing we know for sure is that if you take control of your marriage and the diversions that seem to weaken this relationship, it will make a profound difference in the intimacy you feel for each other. And not only do we speak from a professional experience, but we both speak from the perspective of having been there.

We also know that if you are willing to look at your relationship, evaluate those pressure situations and your personal response, then assess the obstacles you face, you CAN reclaim intimacy in your marriage just as we have. It's going to take some emotional housekeeping and lifestyle changes on your part. Not only are you going to gain a deeper faith in Jesus Christ as you work to become spiritual soulmates, but the communication skills you will learn along with time alone together will give you new energy and strength to deal with life's interruptions, whether minor or monumental.

As you begin this book, take the quiz beginning on page 18 and see how you prioritize those things that affect intimacy with your spouse. Rate yourself according to how frequently the statements are true in your relationship, then continue reading the book for workable ways to overcome specific obstacles in your marriage.

Put Christ in the Center of Your Relationship

At the heart of this book is the reality that true love will always prevail, for a marriage centered in Christ can help you weather any storm. We hold fast to the truth that when two Christians marry, their union should become a living expression of the redemptive relationship of Jesus within the community of believers (the Church).

We will show you how husbands and wives today can learn to love each other with the mutual commitment of Christ and the Church, because the marriage is a celebration of this central mystery of redemption. (See Ephesians 5:21–33.) The bond of marriage is to be a mirror of the bond between Christ and the Church, and it is this bond that becomes real when the couple takes their marriage vows.

No one said that life should be traveled alone. These insightful pages will provide you with great company and allow you to be an active participant in an Intimate Journey that is destined to change your life forever.

Ready to grow? Let's get started!

Wife's Contract

I, _____, understand that I am undertaking an Intimate Journey with my husband _____. I commit myself to this eight-week course to fulfill the requirements of reading and of doing the suggested actions.

Husband's Contract

I, _____, understand that I am undertaking an Intimate Journey with my wife _____. I commit myself to this eight-week course to fulfill the requirements of reading and of doing the suggested actions.

Test Your IQ: Intimacy Quotient

Just how important is your attitude toward intimacy in your marriage? What diversions do you and your spouse face? For Christians, attitude is very important. Paul teaches us to handle conflicts and negative feelings in a positive way: "You are the people of God; he loved you and chose you for his own. So then, you must clothe yourselves with compassion, kindness, humility, gentleness, and patience. Be tolerant with one another and forgive one another whenever any of you has a complaint against someone else. You must forgive one another just as the Lord has forgiven you. And to all these qualities add love, which binds all things together in perfect unity" (Colossians 3:12-14, GNB).

How is your attitude toward intimacy? Rate yourselves according to how frequently the statements are true in your marriage. (Husbands and wives answer separately.)

Scoring:
Always—5 points
Sometimes—3 points
Seldom—1 point
Never—0 points

	W	**H**

1. I never go to bed angry with my spouse, but make amends before we retire. _____ _____

2. I understand the biblical meaning of *agape* love and work to incorporate this unconditional, selfless love into our marriage relationship. _____ _____

3. I attend church regularly and try to incorporate what I have learned into our marriage. _____ _____

4. I work at being a patient and considerate listener. _____ _____

5. I try not to be critical of my partner out loud or in front of our children. _____ _____

6. Sex is not a problem in our relationship. We are responsive to each other's needs and enjoy this part of our life. _____ _____

7. Each day I try to do something kind for my spouse, and to be sensitive to his/her needs. _____ _____

8. Romance is still very much a part of our marriage. We plan special times to keep romance alive. _____ _____

9. We have a close social network of Christian friends from whom we receive support. _____ _____

10. I can express my personal views and opinions to my spouse without fear of being criticized or rejected. _____ _____

11. I spend at least one hour with my spouse each day, talking and sharing my feelings. _____ _____

12. Each day we have a ritual or rou- _____ _____
tine we can count on—having coffee
together in the morning, talking together after dinner alone, going for a
walk, or other.

13. I work to do my share of house- _____ _____
hold chores without being asked or reminded.

14. I basically agree with my spouse on _____ _____
our lifestyle and how our money is
spent.

15. I believe marriage should be a best _____ _____
friendship.

16. I think our sexual relationship _____ _____
should be satisfying to both of us, and
work to do my part in seeing this is true
for us.

17. I tell my spouse daily that I love _____ _____
him/her.

18. We take time each day to walk or _____ _____
exercise.

19. We argue "fairly," not saying or _____ _____
doing things we will regret later on.

20. I deal openly with conflict with _____ _____
my spouse, not keeping it pent up inside.

21. I discuss my feelings freely with my _____ _____
spouse.

22. I pray with my spouse each day. _____ _____

23. When my spouse complains about _____ _____
something, I listen objectively and try
to identify with his/her feelings without resentment.

24. I am careful not to let our children _____ _____
or extended family come between our
relationship as husband and wife.

25. When either of us goes through a _____ _____
crisis, we confront it as a team rather
than as individuals.
26. Divorce is not an option for me. _____ _____
27. I am seeking ways to improve the _____ _____
intimacy in our marriage relationship.

How did you do? Add up your points and see what your score is.

120—135: Congratulations! Continue to do what you are doing and read the next chapters for affirmation and new ideas.

99—119: You're almost there! Look at the areas you are weak in and make plans with your spouse to strengthen these.

75—99: You're working on intimacy. Read on for important growth tips to brush up on those weak areas.

0—74: Wake up! While you may recognize a need for increased intimacy in your marriage, you need to keep reading and apply those suggestions to the weaker areas to make your marriage more satisfying.

1

WEEK ONE

Become Spiritual Soulmates

A successful attorney, Jacob came to see us last year for assistance in strengthening his marriage. This well-educated man had faced the sudden death of his father at the same time that he learned his sixty-eight-year-old mother had terminal cancer. In great need of emotional support, Jacob told how he felt isolated from his wife during these times. "I feel so alone," he said. "Rebecca doesn't seem to understand what I'm going through."

We asked Jacob about his lifestyle and his daily activities. His story was one that we hear often: too much work, too much stress, not enough personal time, no communication or intimacy in his twenty-year marriage, not enough meaningful experiences, and so on.

But Jacob said something else that we need to take seriously. "In trying so hard to make a living, I have neglected my spiritual life."

Aren't we all guilty of that to one degree or another? We get so caught up in the pressures of our goal-oriented society that the only measurement we have of personal fulfillment lies in our wealth and status. Whatever free time we have is often spent staring at the television or burying our head in a mass-market novel. And a society infatuated with material success and results offers no solace. In the midst of our struggle to get ahead, we miss what is most important in life—spiritual wholeness.

As you begin the first week of your Intimate Journey, we encourage you to engage in some serious soul-searching. If you and your spouse are at emotional odds, you are well aware of the anguish it can cause. Perhaps you have blamed your lack of intimacy on the frantic pace of life in the nineties. But experience tells us that if our inner spirit is wrought with turmoil when life's stressors hit, its condition is greatly magnified after doing battle in today's world.

One middle-aged woman told us, "A few weeks after my grandmother died, my father was killed in a car accident. I felt so imperiled as I suffered from feelings of inferiority, loneliness, and, ultimately, burnout. I desperately needed relief and healing but I didn't know where to turn. Mark [her husband] couldn't console me the way I needed comforting."

Discovering Inner Strength

For the past twenty years, as we have talked with couples seeking guidance in how to enhance intimacy in their marriage, we have discovered that one of their main struggles involves the fact that they have ignored their soul, that inner circle of their deepest emotions. Many are dissatisfied with career choices, and with their lives in general. Many suffer low self-esteem from having been abused as children. Others are simply too tired to care about their marriage. On the contrary, we have seen that when both partners have a deep sense of spirituality, they also view life and love differently. And when life's interruptions or crises hit, they meet the challenge in a growth-producing way.

Exploration:

- Name one crisis you have faced this year that has been difficult for you personally. Name one that was difficult for you as a couple.
- What is the one obstacle that is blocking you from becoming a more spiritual person? (fear of the unknown, lack of time, insecurity, other)
- In a crisis or difficult situation that you faced this year, did you turn to Christ Jesus for strength? Why not? If you did turn to him, did you feel relief from life's storm?

Understanding Soulfulness

In *Care of the Soul* (Harper Collins, 1992), theologian Thomas Moore maintains that the soul has to do with genuineness and depth, as when we say certain music has soul, or a remarkable person is soulful. Soulfulness is linked to life in all its particulars—good food, satisfying conversation, genuine friends, and experiences that stay in the memory and touch the heart.

It is our strong conviction that when you care for your soul and nurture your inner spirit, all other areas of life, including emotional intimacy in your marriage, inevitably fall into place. And this care of the soul means giving meticulous attention to our daily actions—what we listen to, what we feel, what we think, and, yes, even how we treat those we love—our husbands and wives.

According to a recent Gallup Poll released by Princeton Religion Research Center, America is rapidly breaking its secular chains and is a nation in recovery. This researcher claims that America has "hit bottom" and is now searching for "spiritual moorings." Gallup notes that not only is the media realizing the importance of religion, but researchers are focusing on the inner life, acknowledging a real connection between prayer and healing, and psychiatry no longer dismisses the importance of religious faith in recovery from emotional illness.

We have experienced that many men and women today are coming to grips with their own mortality—we will not live forever. We have been ambitious, are well-educated, and have material success, but many of us now experience a void or loneliness and a nagging lack of purpose and inner peace. A recent *U.S. News* opinion poll found that 93 percent of all people surveyed believed in God or a universal spirit, and 76 percent of all Americans questioned said that God was a heavenly father, who could be reached through prayer.

Exploration:

- Name a married couple who are spiritual role models to you.
- List some qualities you admire in this couple.

The Christ-Centered Marriage

Four years ago, our friends Janie and Steve told of having no need for God in their busy lives. "Why should we play that 'religion' game?" Janie had said. "Steve has an excellent job, we have a beautiful home, and I'm working on my Master's Degree in psychology. We have everything a couple could ever want."

They had everything until Janie and ten-year-old Meredith were seriously injured in an automobile accident. Then, the very strength they needed in their marriage, a strong faith in

God and each other, was not there. Meredith had severe head injuries, underwent surgery several times over six months, and has diminished vision in one eye; Janie lost the use of her right leg and now uses a walker. Steve? At this writing, he's living alone in an apartment at the beach.

"He couldn't take it that we weren't 'perfect' anymore," Janie told us. "He said he couldn't look at me limping around, and Meredith's problems broke his heart. Everything was great as long as we were unblemished, but now all he does is send a check each month."

If only they had something more . . . before the accident. And that something more is a strong relationship with Jesus Christ who lives in our hearts through faith and grounds us in love. You see, when tragedy struck, Janie and Steve had no spiritual roots to cling to and *no intimate or emotional bond to link them together.*

We know personally how easy it is to become overwhelmed with the stresses of today's society, but taking time to become spiritual soulmates is the basis for a Christ-centered marriage. In our marriage, we lean on the advice given by the apostle Paul in Colossians 3:12–14: "Since you have been chosen by God who has given you this new kind of life, and because of his deep love and concern for you, you should practice tenderhearted mercy and kindness to others. Don't worry about making a good impression on them, but be ready to suffer quietly and patiently. Be gentle and ready to forgive; never hold grudges. Remember, the Lord forgave you, so you must forgive others. Most of all, let love guide your life, for then the whole church will stay together in perfect harmony."

Paul teaches followers of Christ specific behaviors they need to adopt to get along with one another, then he goes one step further and suggests that the word of Christ must dwell within us. It is only then, when "the peace of Christ rules in our hearts," that we can begin to experience intimacy in its deepest form in a Christ-centered marriage.

LOVE is a choice we all must make, whether in our marriages, with our families, at work, at church, or in the community. In everything we do or say, if Christ resides in us, we make the decision to love another person as Christ has loved us.

Exploration:

- Do you feel that your marriage is strongly centered in Christ Jesus? If not, what is keeping you from submitting your relationship to Christ?
- When our basic emotional needs are met through another, we have experienced intimacy. What are some basic emotional needs you have?
- Share how you would like your partner to meet these needs.

Steps to Becoming Spiritual Soulmates

We know that genuine spirituality requires inner renewal rather than outward conformity. Spirituality in a marriage gives meaning and purpose to that relationship.

The steps given in Week One of your Intimate Journey will help you and your spouse to nourish your inner spirits as you delve into a dynamic, forward-looking relationship with Christ Jesus. We have experienced that it is only by first quieting your own the soul, that you can join as spiritual soulmates, reclaiming the emotional intimacy necessary for a meaningful relationship.

Step 1: *Begin with your spiritual journey.*

While many marriage manuals begin with a renewing of the vows or commitment to each other, we feel that to reclaim intimacy in your marriage, you must do some personal homework, plotting your spiritual journey and observing the relationship triggers in your life. This will be done with a journal—preferably a three-ringed notebook with lined paper.

A personal journal can help you and your spouse plot your Intimate Journey and help to uncover your inner selves. Each day you can assess your emotional attitudes, learn how the highs and lows of contemporary life affect both of you and your relationship, and witness how God is working in your lives and in your relationship. These entries should capture your deepest feelings—thoughts that you might not always feel comfortable sharing aloud.

With your thoughts down on paper, you can look back after several weeks and witness your faith and relationship at its highs and lows. The journal can also become an intimate place where you and your spouse can ventilate, meditate, problem-solve, and dream—without feeling threatened or intimidated.

We use a spiritual journal to keep prayer lists, write down answers to prayers, and set goals. We have found that opening up our imagination and reflecting deeply about our spiritual life is important. This means counting our daily blessings and writing these down, naming a moment of happiness and recording this, and getting in touch with our inner spirits as we become more aware of God working through each of us to enhance intimacy in our relationship.

Using the suggested journal for eight weeks (and, hopefully, a lifetime), you and your spouse will keep a log of your responses to daily actions, make observations of these responses, and record your spiritual quest as you discover who you really are—your strengths, weaknesses, personal goals, and intimate needs.

The following excerpt from Jennifer's journal will show you how to organize your own. Use this to gain insight into specific actions, emotional responses, and spiritual awareness that you might experience during your Intimate Journey.

Sample Journal: Week One

Day 1:

Action	Emotional Response	Spiritual Quest
overslept	angry/Jack missed car-pool again.	Give me self-control, Jesus.
Bible study alone	puzzled/lack of understanding	I have so much to learn.
bills came	stunned/We owe that much?	Can you really take care of my needs, Lord?
Mom to doctor	nervous/Test results were positive.	Please heal Mom. family home
Jack napping	harried/TV blasting and kids hungry	Give me self-control, Lord.
doing dishes	resentful/I always have to clean up.	a prayer for forgiveness
time with Jack	lonely/Jack seems preoccupied.	Will we ever reclaim intimacy?
bedtime	tense/My mind won't quit racing.	a prayer for peace

Step 2: *Renew your commitment to Christ.*

For many people, spirituality, imagination, and a faith in God through Jesus Christ have been abstract concepts rather than present realities. Intellectually, we acknowledge that we have a soul, but the reality of it does not have much bearing on how we treat ourselves or our spouse. Now millions say they are seeking an inner dimension to life, spiritual completeness, and intimacy.

Some people serve themselves; we describe them as selfish. Some people serve others; we describe them as altruistic. Jesus Christ offers a higher way. Believers in Christ Jesus live ultimately neither for self nor for others. We live for the glory of God revealed in Christ Jesus. We live to fulfill the will of God. God's will incorporates the welfare of both self and others under a larger, higher standard—the glory of God.[1]

Paul teaches us, "And now just as you trusted Christ to save you, trust him, too, for each day's problems; live in vital union with him. Let your roots grow down into him and draw up nourishment from him" (Colossians 2:6–7). As a couple, we made our marriage vows in the church. From the beginning of that commitment to the present, God is the one who unifies our relationship. The Scripture, "For where two or three gather together because they are mine, I will be right there among them" (Matthew 18:20), is a reality for our relationship. When we affirm God's blessing upon the union of male and female, the marriage ceremony becomes in the fullest sense an instrument of salvation to the couple, their children, and the community of believers who witness their covenant. With God in Christ at the hub of the relationship, all things become possible because of Jesus' love for the Church. This is why Christ must be at the center of all marriage vows, and why the Church must play an important role in all Christian families.

As you renew your commitment to Christ, review the steps given and use the Scriptures to reaffirm this new beginning for you and your spouse in a Christlike relationship.

The following Scriptures will help you know what the Bible says about new life in Christ:

- God loves you (John 3:16; 10:10).
- You are a sinner in need of forgiveness (Romans 3:23; 6:23).
- God wants to forgive you (Romans 5:8; 1 Peter 3:18).

- You must turn away from your sins (Luke 13:5; Ephesians 2:8–9).
- You must place your faith in God's Son, Jesus Christ (Acts 20:21; John 14:6).

As you and your spouse recommit your life to Christ, admit to God that you are a sinner and are turning away from your sins. Place your belief in Jesus Christ, then commit your life to him as you ask him to be your Lord and Savior.

Exploration:

- What are your feelings about a personal relationship with Christ Jesus? How will this affect your marriage? Your career? Your relationship with peers?
- What is the one barrier in your life that hinders your relationship with Christ?

Step 3: *Build your identity: Nurture intimacy with self-care.*

Jean and Stan told us how they realized self-care was necessary before they could love each other. "We each make our own path through life," Jean said. "To succeed and better understand ourselves and our partner, we must be prepared to understand who we are at every stage of the journey and really love that person. Then we can better decide where we want to go—and how to get there."

In a marriage, or any relationship for that matter, self-care is an important factor for loving others. Studies reveal that people who are anchored with a strong faith and a spiritual base feel more secure and have higher self-esteem. Self-care is consistent with a sense of humility, defined by a fourteenth-century monk as "a true knowledge of oneself as one is."[2]

Self-worth is not dependent on external forces, but on a strong internal drive that lets us value who we are without a codependent need for approval from others. As you nurture your relationship with Christ and learn to rest in Him, you will boost your self-esteem so that emotional connectedness with your spouse becomes a reality.

If your self-esteem is low, it is not too late to nurture it. Here are some symptoms of low self-esteem in adults, as well as ways to improve it:

- Often feeling jealous or insecure in relationships.
- Having difficulty giving or accepting compliments.
- Not knowing what you want—from dinner choices to career goals.
- Knowing what you want but not asking for it—in relationships, at work, or at home.
- Rarely expressing your feelings—whether anger, sadness, or love.
- Blaming others for your dissatisfaction or unhappiness.[3]

Once you've identified symptoms of low self-esteem, you can experience inner healing as you take time to nurture yourself—time alone, *away from your spouse*. The gospel has a wealth of insight into the need to be alone. Being alone, as indicated by the life of Jesus, need not be a time for feeling lonely, for we can feel lonely in the midst of a crowd. Being alone can be a time for finding meaning in one's life. When Jesus was in solitude, he found his source of power. After spending the day preaching to and teaching the vast crowds, he "went up on the mountain by himself to pray" (Matthew 14:23, RSV). Luke tells of Jesus spending time teaching and nurturing the people, then he "withdrew to the wilderness and prayed" (Luke 5:16, RSV).

We can become so saturated with church meetings, school commitments, and community obligations that we experience a spiritual void. During these busy times our thoughts can become disorganized, and our relationship with our spouse can seem stifled. This turmoil usually occurs because we did not take time for renewal, to discover our inner resources, or to get our priorities in order while in solitude.

Elizabeth agreed that taking time to be alone—without her husband, Steve—was vital in becoming spiritual soulmates. Why? Alone time is the perfect time for renewal and self-discovery. "When you are in solitude, you can discover what you love most, what makes you feel alive, relaxed, and complete," Elizabeth shared. "During these times of solitude, you can pray, meditate, read the Bible and inspirational books; walk alone on the beach, relax in a hot bath, or set personal goals and be at one with God. It's wonderful to be alone each day because you make a more complete partner for your spouse."

In the book *Living the Adventure*, Keith Miller describes a meeting with the Swiss psychiatrist Paul Tournier. Dr. Tournier shared how he found meaning in his own life through listening to God during moments of being alone. This didn't mean asking God for answers, but rather asking what questions God had for him.

How can God speak to us during these times of spiritual recovery? This is where Christian risk is involved—to be willing to sort through messages and launch out on the ones we feel are of God. The more aware we become of God's presence during alone times through contemplative listening, through Scriptures, and through study, the more real God becomes to us. A communication has begun; a relationship has been sealed.

Suggestions for alone times:

- Read Scriptures; memorize key verses. (See John. 6:15; Luke 22:41; 9:18; Mark 1:35.)
- Take a home study course—books in the Bible or a study of Christian beliefs.
- Go for a nature walk and discover God's creation.
- Learn a new talent or skill, such as sewing, painting, playing the piano.
- Keep prayer lists; study the meaning of prayer.
- Chart your personal and spiritual goals for the day, week, month.
- Read inspirational books or poetry.
- Read a book by a favorite author.
- Do creative writing for personal pleasure.
- Write letters to friends; write letters to people you've wronged, asking for forgiveness.

Step 4: *Commit to spiritual disciplines.*

Becoming a Christian and learning to live like Christ are two completely different matters. When we become a Christian, we acknowledge our innermost need and ask Jesus Christ to live within us and be the Lord of our lives. But to learn about God through Jesus Christ and to grow spiritually, we must make time every day for spiritual disciplines, including Bible study, prayer, meditation, and personal reflection.

Discipline comes from a word that has the same Latin root as *disciple*, which means to "teach and guide." Discipline is variously defined as "training intended to produce a specified character or pattern of behavior" or "the controlled behavior resulting from such training." From another perspective, discipline may be seen as punishment intended to correct or train, or it may be a set of rules or methods. But in the context of the Christian faith, a disciple is not just one who subscribes to the teachings of Jesus and seeks to spread them, but one who seeks to relive Jesus' life in the world. Discipline, for the Christian, is the way we train ourselves or allow the Spirit to train us to be "like Jesus"—to appropriate his spirit and to cultivate his power to live his life in the world.[4]

Commit to a daily prayer life. Prayer is a most important spiritual discipline, as you allow your thoughts to take a break from daily analytical routines and give support to the spiritual dimension of life. When you pray (or meditate), your body is allowed permission to switch from the pumping "fight or flight" response into a calmer, more peaceful mood. Both prayer and meditation provide nourishment for your soul, satiate your spiritual hunger, and help you develop your ability to pay attention to all areas of life without distraction.

As you begin an active prayer life, you must understand that there is a big difference between the *tendency* to pray and the *practice* of prayer. We all have the tendency to pray: the crying out in pain or trouble, the spontaneous shouts of joy. But to live a life of prayer is a different story. To pray consistently is not easy, as it requires commitment and discipline. Don't condemn yourself if you find prayer difficult. Most of us do. Even those whom we call "saints" were said to have found prayer difficult. You can read their journals, and you will find them struggling, searching, wrestling, and seeking to make the tendency to pray a natural practice in everyday life. You may recall that even Jesus' disciples found it difficult to stay awake when Jesus went into the garden to pray.

Prayer is so universal and so natural that its place in our lives needs no defense. We all pray, and we pray because it is a part of our nature. Prayer is related to our search for meaning, our longing for relationship, and our need to grow. Prayer is related to our inborn hunger for God. And prayer is not for God's benefit, but for ours.

Commit to receiving the Christian faith as taught in God's Word. The Bible is central to our understanding of the Christian faith. It teaches us God's plan for our lives as we see in its pages God's love in action. In 2 Timothy 3:16–17, we read that the Bible is God's tool for us to be well-prepared and fully equipped to do good to everyone. The Bible is divinely inspired by God and teaches us what is true, what is right and wrong. And while reading the Bible for *inspiration* is important, Bible *study* is necessary to learn how to apply the Scriptures to our daily lives.

Without the Bible, the Word of God, we would not be the Church. The Old Testament tells us about our past heritage, the New Testament teaches us about Christ and the Church. Understanding the Scriptures, like being a Christian, is also a lifelong process, and we must always be seeking to learn more.

The Bible has one great theme and central figure—Jesus Christ. To know him we need to know God's Word.[5]

Commit to regular worship in Christ's Church. For most of us this hour of worship each week is the time when we shift our burdens from our own shoulders to God's. We find our strength in the Word and people of the Lord.

Not only is church membership important, but regular attendance—as a couple—is vital to our growth in the spiritual disciplines. This means involving ourselves in the life of the church, including Sunday school, Bible studies, music programs, men's and women's groups, worship, and more. The church will enhance our spiritual journey, for it provides training in the Christian faith.

When we join the church, we promise to be faithful to Christ through the church and to live out our commitment through prayer, our presence, our gifts, and our service. This commitment goes beyond attending church once a week; it involves living our faith every day of our lives.

Making a commitment to worship attendance opens the door to a life of strength. New studies show that there is a positive association between religious commitment and our health in later life. Perhaps the most revealing study was done by Duke

University Medical Center, where researchers studied the relationship between religion, aging, and health. This study indicated that one-quarter to one-third of older adults find religion to be the most important factor in enabling them to cope with physical illness and other stresses.

People of faith who attend church frequently have lowered blood pressure and fewer strokes; lower rates of depression, anxiety, and alcoholism; higher life satisfaction and greater well-being; and they adapt better to the rigors of physical illness and disability. Furthermore, religious people perceive themselves as less disabled and experience less pain than do those with similar health problems but without a strong faith in God.[6]

Step 5: *Recognize destructive habits.*

No one has to tell you that emotional reactions to life situations are real. If you are like most of us, just trying to stay afloat can create such anxiety that you lose control of what you say to your spouse. Even inner feelings relay negative messages through body language. Think about it. After an exhausting day at the office or chasing the kids, how do you feel? Emotionally distraught or spiritually complete? You feel a nagging emptiness that you can't pinpoint. So how do you deal with this void? Too often, you take your spiritual emptiness out on your spouse.

We have found that there is a better way to act and react as a Christian couple. Rather than soothing spiritual unrest with emotional outbursts, break the H.A.B.I.T. with the following principles:

- Never allow yourself to get too Harried.
- Never allow yourself to get too Angry.
- Never allow yourself to get too Bored.
- Never allow yourself to get too Intense (or stressed).
- Never allow yourself to get too Tired.

Once you see how your empty spiritual state is motivating negative emotional behaviors, you and your spouse can become free to make lifestyle changes that will affect the intimacy in your marriage in a positive way.

Step 6: *Be open to God's lessons from all of life.*

Spiritual experiences emerge from the most unexpected places. They surprise us and are often recognized only in retrospect. Be open to spiritual growth from any aspect of life. Spiritual lessons can take place while gardening, sitting at the beach watching the sunset, listening to the choir sing during worship, playing with your children, as well as praying together.[7]

As you and your spouse take time from your daily routine to nurture your spiritual lives together, you will tap the reservoirs of peace, strength, and assurance that are available to those who follow Christ. When you feel like your world is caving in around you and you long for a fortress, a refuge, being bonded together in a Christ-centered marriage will give you the strength to reach out to your unshakable source of strength—Christ himself. The grace of an omnipotent God and the power and love that are in Christ Jesus, reach beyond what we can ever expect from ourselves and our human resources.

Our bodies, minds, and spirits need the opportunity to celebrate our existence, to look within and find meaning in being a unique child of God as we slow down and take time out to celebrate our spirituality together.

The time-outs may be as uncomplicated as

- reflecting together on a brilliant sunrise;
- sharing a cup of tea or coffee in the backyard, watching birds and small wildlife;
- meditating as you enjoy a peaceful painting or poem;
- screening your phone calls to allow time together for Bible

study, prayer, or spiritual reflection;
- or going on a quiet moonlit walk.

Week One: Become Spiritual Soulmates

Focus: Week One on your Intimate Journey will allow you to discover the intimate feelings you have when you acknowledge your soul—your spirituality. Each week you will read the appropriate chapter, then use the following actions—one for each day of the week—to tie in what you have learned with your new lifestyle in Christ. The following actions are designed to be done with your spouse, but if your spouse cannot participate, they can also be done alone.

Central Bible Truth: "For where two or three gather together because they are mine, I will be right there among them" (Matthew 18:20).

Monday: *Start your spiritual journal.*

While life's difficult journey can leave us feeling fragmented and lost, journaling provides a framework we can use to piece life back together during stressful times—and these are stressful times! Ultimately, gaining new perspective in life leads to greater creativity and spiritual depth.

In the journal, you will begin to discover your "enemy within"—negative beliefs that hold you back from celebrating *who you are and whose you are.* These beliefs have become a part of us through the years from our parents, our friends, our enemies, our society, maybe even our church, and they often keep us from being *fully alive.* Once these beliefs have been identified for what they are, we can be free to discover positive affirmations about ourselves and our partner—positive truths that will build the intimacy in our marriage.

Reflection and response:

Begin your eight-week journal today with your spouse. In separate notebooks, use the headings as given on page 30, and write down today's observations in your notebook. Talk with your spouse about these before bedtime, then write down your feelings here:

_____

_____

_____

His: _____

_____

Hers: _____

_____

Tuesday: *Name your spiritual experiences.*

How did you see God act in your life today? Stop and notice!

Reflection and response:

With your husband or wife, get in the habit of naming your daily spiritual experiences by asking,

- *What did I do today that was of God?* (Examples: helped a friend, volunteered, comforted a co-worker, listened to a child.)
- *What did I see today that was of God?* (Examples: a colorful sunrise, the smile of a friend, new blossoms on flowers, the contentment of my spouse.)

- *What did I think today that was of God?* (Examples: loving thoughts, empathetic thoughts, thoughts of passion, benevolent thoughts.)
  Write down some of your spiritual experiences here:

His: _____

_____

Hers: _____

_____

Wednesday: *Focus on Bible study.*

The Bible is the one book that must be worn to be effective in the life of the reader. Georgianna Summers in *Teaching As Jesus Taught* suggests that we place an exclamation mark (!) for ideas that we find exciting, a question mark (?) for ideas that need clarification, an upward arrow (▲) for anything that seems to tell us "Do this," and a downward arrow (▼) for the message "Stop doing this."[8]

Reflection and response:

Write down ideas revealed today while studying the Scriptures that motivated you to take specific action in your life, whether in changed behavior, thoughts, or speech. How do these actions relate to your marriage relationship?

His: _____

_____

Hers: _____

_____

Thursday: *Begin a life of prayer.*

Prayer provides nourishment for your soul, satiates that "inner" spiritual hunger, and helps you develop your relationship with a loving Father who can heal distraught relationships. It is often impossible to connect emotionally with anyone when your inner spirit is "soul sick."

Today, call upon the reservoirs of peace, strength, and assurance that are available to you in Christ. If your world is caving in around you or you feel overwhelmed or distraught, reach out together with your spouse for your unshakable source of strength—Christ himself.

Reflection and response:

How should you pray? Some people pray as they work each day; some pray with songs; others pray while kneeling in a quiet room. The only expert on prayer is God—ask *him* how you should pray.

With your spouse, write down a sentence prayer using the ACTS formula, specifically thanking God for your spouse. A sample is done for you:

His:

Adoration: Lord, I praise you for the gift of love that I share with Ginny.

Confession: I confess that I sometimes ignore her, especially when I'm preoccupied.

Thanksgiving: You know that she means more to me than anything, and I thank you for this chance to become more intimately connected with her.

Supplication: Christ Jesus, I ask for your hand upon me when I become preoccupied, to guide me into getting to know my wife as a child of God.

His:

Adoration _____

_____

Confession _____

_____

Thanksgiving _____

_____

Supplication _____

_____

Hers:

Adoration _____

_____

Confession _____

_____

Thanksgiving _____

_____

Supplication _____

_____

Friday: *Break emotional outbursts.*

We have become too serious about life—too tense, too stressed. We equate maturity with seriousness and believe wisdom comes to us only through sober reflection and long-considered judgment.[9] It should not be that way, for we know that when we are stressed, we usually take it out on those around us.

How do you react when you feel empty, lonely, and misunderstood? Many couples release negative emotions by arguing, name-calling, or even ignoring the other.

As we discussed on page 38, we have found that there is a better way to act and react as a Christian couple, by breaking the H.A.B.I.T., rather than soothing spiritual unrest with emotional outbursts. Review the principles again and talk about how these behaviors affect your relationship.

Reflection and response:

Do an attitude check today and write down specific times of negativism or emotional and hurtful outbursts that were caused by being too harried, angry, bored, intense or stressed, or too tired. How can you protect your marriage from such outbursts?

His: _____

_____

Hers: _____

_____

Saturday: *Take time off—together.*

Marcus Aurelius said, "A man's life is what his thoughts make it." Today we want you to take a break from your daily analytical routine and give support to the spiritual dimension of your lives. This time away from distressing situations will allow your bodies, minds, and spirits to experience healing.

Reflection and response:

After you and your partner have been alone—away from your home—for a period of time, write down how you feel without the daily intrusions of ringing phones, doorbells, TV, and children.

His: _____

_____

Hers: _____

_____

Sunday: *Review your week.*

On Day 7 of your Intimate Journey, we want you to review the notes you both have made in this chapter along with the spiritual insights gathered in your journal. Do you see a parallel between your spiritual life and your emotional responses to your spouse? You can identify this relationship as you observe the situations encountered during days 1–6 and your emotional and spiritual responses.

Reflection and response:

While the inward essence of Christianity lies in faith, its external expression is love. At the heart of Christian love is self-giving, and that is what you will talk about today.[10] Write down insights you have gathered about your spiritual life, including specific needs you should work on individually and together (more Bible study, a regular commitment to the church, quieting the inner spirit, and so on).

His:_____

_____

Hers _____

_____

2

WEEK TWO
Recharge Your Best Friendship

"And this is Deb, my best friend." That's how Bob introduced me at the alumni dinner several years ago. My initial response was anything but appreciative as other members had used such romantic terms as "my beautiful better half" and "the love of my life." When Bob said the words "best friend," I envisioned him describing one of his golfing pals. Yet as he sat down, I decided that perhaps I had been paid the highest compliment a wife could receive, especially as he leaned over and whispered, "You are my best friend! I'd rather be with you than anyone else."

We are really intrigued by best friendships in marriage, especially how two very different people can be married, stay in love, and keep alive that special liking for each other day after day, year after year. While the dictionary describes a friend as "a person whom one knows well," to experience a best friendship takes time, energy, and constant nurturing.

This ongoing care seeks only good for the other; it's the

same self-giving *agape* love described in the Gospels. Jesus taught "the greatest love is shown when a person lays down his life for his friends" (John 15:13). The Bible continues to speak often of friendships. "A true friend is always loyal, and a brother is born to help in time of need (Proverbs 17:17). And, "Don't just think about your own affairs, but be interested in others, too, and in what they are doing" (Philippians 2:4).

But even with the encouragement we have from the Bible, for intimacy to strengthen within a marriage, friendships must be constantly nourished—even when you don't feel like it—and that is the challenge you will undertake this week in your Intimate Journey.

Love Is Not a Feeling

"But some days I just don't feel in love with Mark," Shannon told us. "Especially after a long day at work, I don't feel loving at all."

To which we asked, "Who said that love was just a feeling?"

As you begin to take steps to recharge the best friendship with your husband or wife, it is important to know upfront that loving someone is something we do even when we don't "feel" like it.

When we met more than twenty-four years ago, we were attracted to each other by qualities that made us unique. My (Deb) enthusiasm for life and creativity intrigued Bob; I appreciated Bob's keen insight and musical talents. Our marriage has been one of being soulmates rather than "role mates." We have seen problems arise in many relationships in which men and women attempt to fit their spouses into neat roles and expect them to perform accordingly, instead of rejoicing in their spouse's uniqueness. How much better it would be to bury expectations and relate to the individual we love as the remarkable, singularly unique person that he or she is—a person who will never come this way again.[1]

As we have experienced, people are drawn to each other because of their differences. But no sooner do we fall in love than we set about trying to change the very elements about each other that make us different. We try to make our mates more like ourselves.

This is often a losing proposition. People resent being asked to change, and resentment undermines intimacy.[2] It has been said that a marriage is like a business partnership. In a marriage, successful friends, like business partners, build on these natural differences to create something more interesting and more precious than either of them could have created on their own.[3]

Bob affirms this new creation when he performs marriage ceremonies and closes the ceremony by introducing the couple, saying, "Brothers and sisters in Christ, I now present to you a new creation of God, something that never existed before . . . Mr. and Mrs. Smith, Joe and Alice." This one statement signifies the uniqueness of uniting two very different individuals to create a new whole.

Intimacy means that we can each be who we are in a relationship. Being a unique person in Christ requires that we talk openly about things that are important to us, that we take a clear position on where we stand on important emotional issues, and that we clarify the limits of what is acceptable and what is tolerable to us in a relationship. Allowing the other person to do the same means we can stay emotionally connected to our partner who thinks, feels, and believes differently, without needing to change, convince, or fix the other.[4]

Exploration:

- Name a recent time when you felt like best friends with your marriage partner.
- What hinders this friendship from being a reality daily?
- What is one thing you could do to encourage friendship in your marriage?
- How are you and your partner different? The same? Can you see how your differences complement each other?

Common Stumbling Blocks in Marriages Today

Not surprisingly, many marriages, even those performed in Christ's church, have not experienced an intimate relationship centered in Christ; in fact, many seem doomed the moment the vows are spoken. Some of these individuals have experienced stumbling blocks that forecast destruction early on in the relationship, before marriage is even considered.

Some of the most common obstacles that restrict intimacy and even friendship in marriages include the following:

Communication problems. Communication is a vital ingredient in intimate relationships, but some couples cannot relate to each other in a loving and meaningful manner no matter how hard they try. (See Chapter 3.) Intimacy is marked by very close association and warm friendship. But how can you be emotionally connected if you cannot share your feelings?

Marriage partners can choose to be intimate and communicate their joys, fears, goals, and dreams, or they can choose to step back and be distant in the relationship. By being open about our feelings with our spouse, we allow for full acceptance and understanding.

Self-centeredness. Many consider the "I" more important than the "we" in a marriage. Excessive spending on individual wants, leaving the partner often to be with other friends, or becoming absorbed with a personal agenda at the cost of sacrificing the marriage unit are some symptoms of a serious lack of intimacy. Intimate bonding cannot take place where one or both partners are absorbed in self-interests.

Pride. This is evident when a spouse cannot or will not admit to being wrong, or fails to offer the forgiveness that Jesus taught. Unconditional forgiveness is most essential in an intimate relationship. Carrying a grudge for past mistakes will kill any hopes of emotional connectedness.

Low self-esteem. Intimate love is confident love, not to be confused with selfishness. High self-esteem means that you know your value as a child of God, and that you are worthy of being loved. Persons entering into a marriage with low self-esteem will have difficulty participating in a truly intimate relationship.

Disillusionment. This occurs when a marriage partner is not as he or she appeared prior to the marriage ceremony, or when he or she reneges on issues previously agreed upon. Even though a relationship suffering from disillusionment can be restored through counseling and developing new trust and confidence, many couples erect defenses for their behavior, blocking any hope of intimacy.

Immaturity. One partner may have achieved greater maturity before the marriage than the other and can therefore cope better with stresses within the marriage. When the husband cannot take appropriate leadership because of immaturity, this can lead to resentment on the part of the wife, or vice versa, when the wife is immature with regard to dealing with small disappointments or unmet expectations.

Lifestyle expectations. Both individuals come into the marriage with certain expectations of how and where they want to live—the neighborhood, the home, the car they drive, vacations, weekends, entertainment—but if one of the partners is disappointed with an aspect of the lifestyle, intimacy will be threatened.

Refusal to compromise. Many couples stay at odds because they cannot handle "losing" an argument or giving in to their spouse. We are called to love and accept our partner and this means wanting the best for the other. Intimacy requires compromise and negotiation to remain strong.

Inability to set limits. One partner may work long hours while the other sits at home waiting, without communication. An inability to manage time and set limits can extend into after-work hours as well—excessive volunteering in the community, constantly being with friends rather than your spouse, or becoming child-centered rather than family-centered or focusing proportionately on the marriage can all contribute to a lack of intimacy. In order to be intimate, both partners must set aside time to be alone with each other on a regular basis.

Background differences. We are each a product of our past, our families, our environment. Partners coming from different backgrounds, including religious practices, beliefs about the role of men and women in marriage, socioeconomic levels, and educational training, will experience problems that hinder intimacy unless these issues are discussed and some agreement or compromise concerning them is reached.

Exploration:

- What stumbling blocks do you face in your relationship? Not enough time? Too many work responsibilities? More month than money? Out-of-control children? Write down three stumbling blocks you face:

His:

1. _____

2. _____

3. _____

Hers:

1. _____

2. _____

3. _____

- Of the stumbling blocks listed, circle the ones that you feel are most crucial to resolve before intimacy can be reached or increased. Put a line through the ones that are not as important to your relationship as a couple.

Marriage Is God's Idea

For those who may believe that marriage is something human beings thought up, we must inform you, it is not so. Marriage is God's idea, not man's. In Ephesians 5:31 we read, "A man shall leave his father and mother and be joined to his wife, and the two shall become one flesh" (RSV). This affirms what we know to be true, that a Christ-centered marriage will have a spiritual dimension that is in the world, yet not of the world. It is this spiritual dimension—intimacy—that enhances the passionate and physical oneness in the relationship.

Paul taught that Christians are different, and the one thing that distinguishes them from others in the secular world is love. Paul was so convinced of the power of love that he said if people loved God and others, everything else in life would fall into place. This unconditional love described in the Bible is offered to us now, right where we are in life—weaknesses and all.

The Bible tells us that Christian love is different than other forms of love. *Philio* (a mutual friendship) and *eros* (an erotic, but selfish desire) can begin a love relationship, but will not stand the test of time alone. Mutual friends can disagree and fall away, beauty or sexual appeal will diminish. The apostle Paul spoke of *agape* love, which is self-giving, filled with compassion and empathy. This love seeks the best for others, is unconditional, caring, and benevolent.

Agape love is consistent with intimate love. It continues to care and show compassion for the other—even when that person is broken, faces problems, is ill, or acts unlovely. Agape love or intimate love never changes! And that is the kind of love we are called to have in our marriages today.

Exploration:

- What attracted you to your spouse?
- Were you best friends before you became romantically involved?
- What types of love describe your relationship today?

Steps to Developing a Best Friendship

Ralph Waldo Emerson said, "The only way to have a friend is to be one." And being a friend with your husband or wife takes time and effort.

All of us bring to our intimate relationships certain expectations. While we may want loyalty, companionship, and friendship, aren't we afraid we might get the exact opposite if we become too intimately involved with our partner? That is where risk taking and faith come in.

As you start the following steps to recharge your best friendship and begin a step-by-step maintenance plan, it is important to enter in with an open mind and a willing heart—so that a deeper friendship and more intimate relationship can grow.

Step 1: *Make times to be together.*

Mother Teresa once said, "Loneliness and the feeling of being unwanted is the most terrible poverty."[5] Too many of us have taken the "external trip" in our marriages and our lives. Our energies have been directed toward collecting things, being the wealthiest, the biggest, and the best. Now we have most of the things we need for comfort, but they haven't gotten us very far. We are basically still very lonely, many of us are lost, and most of us are confused.[6]

In one survey, more than half of the 40,000 people surveyed reported that they sometimes or often felt lonely. This suggests that loneliness affects more than 100 million Americans, including married couples. Simply put, being married does not protect you from feeling lonely.

Relationships do not grow or remain stimulating without conscious effort; we must take time to enrich our lives, and therefore our love, or we are merely coexisting. Complacency kills.[7] You can help your relationship grow by taking time each day to be with your partner—alone. You might allow a period during the evening hours to touch base with your husband or wife, or make a point to meet for lunch during a busy workday. Talk about your partner's interests—and listen!

What is he saying?

Is she lonely?

Does he need a listening ear?

Is your husband hurting due to work conflict or inner turmoil?

Does your wife need time out to discover her inner potential?

Try to read between the lines while talking, and relate a message of caring. Remember the apostle Paul's words: "Don't just think about your own affairs, but be interested in others, too, and in what they are doing."

Take time out from the children. Get a baby-sitter. Go for a drive, a walk, to a park, or out to dinner. The first few minutes may seem uncomfortable, but the longer you are together without caring for the children, the more relaxed you both will become.

Make a standing commitment with a baby-sitter every Friday or Saturday night. Just knowing that someone else will care for the children will let you relax and enjoy each other, even if you don't go anywhere. Put a mandatory expenditure in your grocery budget or miscellaneous household budget. Once you have allocated this, use it every week to do something together.

Step 2: *Celebrate your differences.*

You're neat; he's not. He's a hugger; you're not. Intimate marriages are the merging of two very different partners. If you love someone, your goal is to want them to be all that they are, and you will encourage them every inch of the way. You will do everything to help them become more, then you will dance and celebrate the occasion. You're not growing apart, you are growing together, but hand and hand—not melting one into the other.

After one month of marriage, we experienced a rude awakening about how very different we were when we tried to combine our personal body clocks. According to popular marriage surveys, our relationship really shouldn't work. Some attest that marriages where one person likes to stay up late and the other person retires early and gets up early are just not compatible. One study stated that in these marriages there wasn't enough time for private conversation, the communication that should take place in a marriage was stilted, and the two different body clocks created unharmonious rhythms.

Now we don't like to dispute the experts, but let's be realistic. Can a morning "lark" really be happily married to a nocturnal animal? We know so! Let us give you an example of how our body clocks find harmony.

Deb:

It is 5:00 A.M. My eyes pop wide open without the assistance of an alarm. After all, it is another gorgeous day and there is so much to do. I hear Bob breathing deeply as he sleeps next to me, and I quietly tiptoe out of the bedroom. The birds chirping at daybreak add a cheerful sound as I pour my hot early morning coffee. Then I celebrate; it's "my time." Two hours . . . I have two wonderful hours to read, pray, write, and think clearly before anyone else awakens. You see, the early-bird hours are the time in my day that I spend alone with God. As I unload the dishwasher, make school lunches, dust a table or two, and fold last night's laundry, I am constantly thinking of ideas, stopping to make a list or two, and asking God to give direction to the day.

Now as delightful as this time is, all good things sadly come to an end. About 3:00 each afternoon, my body slowly, but surely, begins to tire. My mind becomes a bit foggy, and the great, creative ideas are less frequent. I put all big projects on hold for the day and begin to focus on family duties—kids home from school, car-pools to run, a last-minute errand, dinner to cook, dishes to clean, and homework to monitor.

Now, let's turn back the clock to see how Bob, the "night owl," approaches the day.

Bob:

The alarm rings for three loud minutes before I finally turn it off. 7:30 A.M. It seems like the middle of the night to me—the devoted nocturnal animal—but seeing the daylight pouring in my window, I know it is a reality. I usually stumble out of bed, bump into a wall or two, and finally turn on the shower to help signal my aging body to wake up.

Family members are greeted with a barely audible "Good morning." Breakfast is eaten while reading the paper . . . not too much conversation yet. A quick kiss and my blurry eyes guide me to the car. Another day has begun.

I spend my early mornings at the office in study, then begin to see parishioners after 9:30 A.M., once my body has realized that the owner really did wake it up.

Now here is where our real differences begin. By 9:30 A.M. Deb has already edited several manuscripts, written an outline or two for articles, vacuumed the bedrooms, wiped down the bathrooms, and started early dinner preparations. By 9:30 A.M. Bob has settled into his office and has started to open his mail from the previous day. By 3:00 in the afternoon, Deb is winding down from her busy day. By 3:00, Bob has just finished a luncheon meeting and is starting his afternoon schedule.

At 7:30, we pause and celebrate our lives together. As the children work in their rooms, we sit in the den and talk about our respective days. Deb's mind is through being creative, so she can think about Bob's needs and dreams. Bob's mind has not fully clicked into the creative mode, so he can think about Deb's needs and dreams. We talk about children and family and bills and vacation. We argue about politics and current events and teenage curfews and the neighbor's barking dog. We hug and kiss and smile and laugh. We joke and cry and pray and sit in solitude. Yes, nix the studies; we are compatible.

It is 9:30 P.M. The children have all been tucked in. Their lights are all out. Deb is now ready for bed mentally and physically. Her mind is tired, her body aches, and the cool covers look so inviting. As she turns off the light by the bed, Bob kisses her good-night and tiptoes back into the den.

Now, let the good times roll. This is Bob's time. He thinks and creates. He plans and reads. He makes prayer lists, job lists, and visitation lists. He tinkers with a new program on the computer, throws in a load of wash, watches the news, and listens to his new CD. He quietly plays the piano in the distant living room, hums the verse to a new hymn, and prays aloud. He is alive, vibrant, creative, and, yes, very awake.

The mantel clock strikes midnight, and Bob reminds his body that it has to be tired. Finally, his day is done as he turns back the covers on the bed and crawls in.[8]

Differences do complement intimacy. Perhaps it is our strong independence that keeps our marriage together. After all, if we had the same body clock, we might not have those times for aloneness and creative thinking. But more than that, we know that people who are different in some ways can fill voids in your life. Deb's cheerfulness during the morning hours gets the family off the ground and moving. Bob's energy at night helps complete our busy day when the family's needs change. Despite the conclusions of modern science, we still claim the Scripture "For where two or three gather because they are mine, I will be right there among them" (Matthew 18:20). His love—not our "compatibility"—is the basis for our relationship.

Step 3: *Observe your behavior.*

Learn to step outside yourself in your marriage by focusing on how your partner perceives you. Listen to what you say to your spouse. Watch how you act and react to what he says. Use this process of observation to make much-needed changes in your relationship, as you begin to treat your spouse as a best friend.

After you have made observations, make changes. Challenge your interpretation of love as you open the door to new possibilities in your relationship.

Exploration:

Actions speak much louder than words. While we affirm the need to say the words "I love you," we also believe that it is important to show by actions that you love the other:

- Straighten a collar.
- Give a kiss on the cheek when least expected.
- Call him or her at work for no reason except to say "I'm thinking about you."
- Place a note under your partner's pillow telling him how much he means to you.
- Bring home her favorite candy.
- Slip up from behind and give your partner a loving hug.
- Pick out his tie in the morning.
- Give her a back rub before bedtime.

Write down three loving actions you would like your spouse to do for you:

His

1. _____

2. _____

3. _____

Hers

1. _____

2. _____

3. _____

Step 4: *Treat your spouse as your best friend.*

The best way to have a friend is to be a friend. And this saying applies to married couples as well as to friendships outside of marriage. Before you do or say something that may be hurtful, ask yourself, Would I say or do this to my best friend? So many times we don't hold our tongue, and we say mean things to the person we love because we think he or she ought to understand and love us no matter what.

Trust and caring are vital to this best friendship between husband and wife. According to John Gray, Ph.D., author of *Men Are From Mars, Women Are From Venus*,[9] men strongly need to feel trusted. One of the most loving messages a man can receive is "I'll leave you alone to do this by yourself." Such a comment tells him his competence is trusted.

On the other hand, a woman needs to feel cared for. To her, a high degree of involvement is a sign of love. Most women love shared projects and assistance with a task.[10]

Think back to the last time you and your partner argued. Ask yourself, Would I have said those same words to a close friend? An acquaintance? Starting today you can do something positive to counteract all the grumbling and disagreements you and your spouse have had by focusing on the other. Turn your energy toward caring for your spouse in the manner of a best friend by watching your speech, your actions, your body language, your tone of voice, and your thoughts. While this may sound too easy to work, it will work to rebuild the bridge that joins you together.

Step 5: *Stop destructive criticism.*

Criticism makes us feel inadequate and rejected. In Paul's letters to the people of Corinth, he affirmed their strong points while also pointing out areas of their Christian life that needed improvement. Perhaps many of the Corinthians were highly offended by his statements, but Paul wrote to them in a true spirit of Christian love, urging unity and acceptance of one another. Paul allowed for differences of opinions and gifts while encouraging harmony in Christ.

As we focus on the gospel challenge of agape love in our marriages, we need to focus on finding remedies for problems rather than dwelling on who is at fault. Realizing that criticism, even from well-meaning husbands and wives, is often painful, we can use it to become more caring toward others. Are we too critical of our spouses? Let the Scripture in John 8:7—"But only he who never sinned may throw the [stones] first"—be your guide as you interact with others. Thinking before we speak can help us learn to be less critical.

If you feel the need to criticize your spouse, always count to ten before you speak. Ask, How would I like to be told this? Also, ask yourself if the criticism is going to help this person grow or is it just your opinion? To build intimacy in marriage, avoid sharing criticism that may destroy your partner's self-esteem.

Exploration:

Jesus taught, "Never criticize or condemn—or it will all come back on you. Go easy on others; then they will do the same for you" (Luke 6:37). Keep this Scripture in mind as you and your spouse work on watching how you throw critical statements at each other.

Step 6: *Forgive and forget.*

An inability to forgive and forget (wrongdoings and personal hurts) guarantees a source of perpetual pain and chronic misery.[11] We all make mistakes in our lives; no one is innocent of this. A true friend is able to forgive the other and move on to a closer relationship. A true friend in a marriage is also able to accept the forgiveness of the other, which is often the more difficult thing to do.

Simply put, forgiveness is the whole essence of the Gospels. And this forgiveness should be a part of our caring relationship with our spouse. We have the potential in our marriage to make changes in our lives—both separately and together. We need to forgive and forget, to erase the slate and begin again.

God forgives and he wants us to forgive. Forgiveness is not natural, but forgiveness and other biblical virtues are unique because they reflect God's character. God enables his people to forgive. He wants us to possess virtues that are a part of his Person. Failure to forgive closes the door to our own forgiveness and opens the door to hatred, abuse, fear, and other destructive responses.[12]

Exploration:

- Do you need forgiveness for past mistakes?
- Have you asked your partner to forgive you?

Step 7: *Be supportive.*

Stand up for your partner. We learn in Proverbs that "A true friend is always loyal, and a brother is born to help in time of need" (Proverbs 17:17). When you are your partner's best friend, you believe in him/her no matter what happens. This often means going to "bat" for him when job trials are overwhelming or for her when raising children becomes a tedious daily chore. Some marriage partners only pretend to be friends.

Yet a true friend is loyal and takes risks in supporting the other. A true friend in a marriage doesn't hesitate to stick up for the other.

Exploration:

- How do you need support in your marriage?
- Are you getting this from your partner?
- How do you feel when you don't feel supported?
- Write down one way you have supported your partner today.

Week Two: Recharge Your Best Friendship

Focus: Friendships, even in a marriage, can often become one-sided. That's why it is important to make time to be together; to communicate your personal joys and concerns; to share your faith in God, your ups and downs, your goals and fears. As you take time to build an honest marriage-friendship relationship, you will both become more sensitive to each other's inner needs. Paul teaches in Galatians 6:2, "Share each other's troubles and problems, and so obey our Lord's command." Let your relationship be a refueling station for you and your spouse as you work on the following actions.

Central Bible Truth: "We know what real love is from Christ's example in dying for us. And so we also ought to lay down our lives for our Christian brothers" (1 John 3:16).

Monday: *Make time for friendship.*

Take a few minutes during the day to touch base with your spouse, either by phone or in person. Also allow a period during the evening to talk one-on-one; talk about his or her interests—and listen. Find out what bothers him, what he dreams about, and what he fears. Go further and read between the lines. Does your spouse say that all is okay, yet seems lonely inside? Does she lack confidence in herself? These insights are important because they give clues to interpersonal behavior and actions. Don't forget that empathy is understanding the other person's point of view. This does not mean that we must accept the other's view, but we must be willing to try to understand it.

Reflection and response:

Send a note to your spouse through the mail today or put it in a place where he or she can find it—a briefcase, purse, or under his pillow. In the note, affirm your spouse and tell him why he is special to you. Lift up a special quality that she has and praise her for this. Write down the feelings you had when you sent this personal note and when you received a love note from your spouse.

His: _____

_____

Hers: _____

_____

Tuesday: *Create a ritual.*

To strengthen the emotional closeness with your spouse, you will need to launch out in faith and believe that no matter how difficult it is, you and your spouse can grow together. Successful friends, like successful business partners, build on their natural differences to create something more interesting and more fragile than either one of them could have created on his or her own.[13]

Rituals or traditions are important for increasing the emotional bond between two very different people, especially in our transient, fast-paced society where intimacy in marriage is uncommon. Rituals for married couples offer a sense of identity in an impersonal world; they bond the partners to one another, helping them to maintain a stability that will carry them through when they face trials in their lives in the home and outside the home.

Reflection and response:

Set up a new ritual for you and your spouse that includes together time. This could be waking up a bit earlier to have coffee, or staying up after the kids are tucked in to share favorite music or a dessert. We always spend at least an hour together each evening just talking—without the telephone, TV, or teens. Friday night is also our sacred time, set aside ritually to be alone, go out to dinner, or enjoy a video together—no phone, no kids—just the two of us.

We have found that rituals enhance intimacy in marriage, especially if it is something you can look forward to on a regular basis. Rituals will add to the dependability of your marriage and increase your trust in each other.

His: _____

_____

Hers: _____

_____

Wednesday: *Forgive your spouse.*

For most of us, showing humility toward our spouse while asking for forgiveness is not easy, but laying aside self-pride is essential to any loving relationship. (Read Philippians 2:1–9.)

Reflection and response:

Openly say the words "I'm sorry" today for something that has been standing between you. The best way to admit that you were wrong is to be genuine and upfront with your spouse. Encourage your spouse to interject his feelings and talk about how much God has forgiven us and how we are to forgive each other. (Read Matthew 18:21–34 together.)

His: _____

_____

Hers: _____

_____

Thursday: *Define your expectations.*

By now you have certainly thought of special needs or expectations you might have of your partner as you strengthen your emotional bond and increase intimacy. Aristotle described friendship as "one soul in two bodies." That is the goal of this exercise as you experience the give-and-take of ideas.

Reflection and response:

While you are alone with your spouse, identify five specific expectations you have of your relationship, and write these in the space below. Have your spouse do the same and write these next to yours. Talk about these expectations in a manner that does not hurt your partner but opens up new lines of communication. Listen carefully to your partner's response, trying to feel what he or she feels. Then respond in a kind and caring manner as you begin goal setting in your relationship.

Intimate Expectations

His	Hers
1. _____	1. _____
2. _____	2. _____
3. _____	3. _____
4. _____	4. _____
5. _____	5. _____

Friday: *Talk about your intimate expectations.*

After you have written out your intimate expectations, sit with your spouse and talk about these personal needs without criticizing him or her or bringing up the past. You need to focus on this day and the days to come and let the past be finished.

Do not say:

"You have never been compassionate before, and that is what I need."

Instead, say:

"I hope we can build on the compassion in our marriage."

Do not say:

"I hope now you will finally make some time for me."

Instead, say:

"I look forward to spending more time with you."

Do not say:

"I've never really trusted you; I hope I can start now."

Instead, say:

"Let's build on the trust we have for each other."

Reflection and response:

Remember, what you say (or don't say) affects any hope for intimacy you might have. Be honest with your needs and feelings, but be tactful! Tact is that delicate perception of knowing the right thing to say or do without offending your spouse. When a person uses tact in sharing feelings without distorting the truth in any way, growth can occur. You use tact in your marriage relationship because you care about the other person and how he or she feels. This involves speaking the truth with hopes of preserving the intimate relationship rather than tearing it apart.

Confiding in your spouse with your innermost feelings is the first step in getting in touch with the emotions that can keep your marriage alive.

Saturday: *Take responsibility for friendship.*

In 1 John 3:18 it says, "Little children, let us stop just *saying* we love people; let us *really* love them, and *show it* by our *actions*." Our love must not be merely words and fine talk. It must be expressed in action and sincerity. Best friendships depend on active love. Spend time today taking responsibility for your best friendship. Remember, the goal of a best friendship is to find remedies for problems in the relationship rather than dwell on who is at fault.

Reflection and response:

M. Scott Peck wrote, "Passion is a deception created by nature to bring people together. It is wonderful when it's there, but the real, hard work in developing a relationship comes after the passion abates, through the process of undertaking responsibilities and commitments through recognizing and accepting that you and your spouse are two very different people sharing one life."[14]

Look for ways to be sensitive to your spouse today, instead of impulsively issuing demands or criticisms. Even silence can be taken negatively. Make sure your response is affirming. Write down how you feel when you are treated respectfully.

His: _____

_____

Hers: _____

_____

Sunday: *Share joys and concerns with your partner.*

Friendships can become one-sided. Especially in a marriage, one spouse may become more of a listener to the problems of the other. In order for you and your spouse to become intimately bonded, both of you must communicate personal joys and concerns with the other. As you take time to build an honest and mutual relationship, you will each become more sensitive to the needs of the other.

Reflection and response:

The Christian walk is a walk of faith. Spend some time sharing your faith in God, your ups and downs, your goals and fears. Let your spouse know of some past struggles in your life. Write in the blanks how you feel when you hear your spouse's innermost concerns. How did you feel sharing yours?

His: _____

_____

Hers: _____

_____

3

WEEK THREE

Cease Fire! Break the Ice With Communication

Most of us will never forget the moment: After years of preparation, frustration, and tremendous cost overruns, the spaceship Columbia sat poised on launch pad #39 ready for lift-off. Millions watched around the world. But then, suddenly and unexpectedly, the countdown was halted. Everything stood still. Finally, we watched in disappointment as the astronauts climbed back down out of the cabin and the entire launch was delayed for two days. Why? Because two computers couldn't talk to each other!

Who hasn't dealt with computer problems, whether on the job or at home? We're used to their erratic and unpredictable behavior. But what about in your marriage? What happens when communication between a married couple stops altogether?

Communication is a tough business, and nowhere is it any tougher than in a marriage. But, as you will learn in week three of your Intimate Journey, communication is necessary in order for marriages to thrive. Communication is so important that a popular mass-market magazine polled over 30,000 women and only one marriage problem ranked above conflicts over money: poor communication. One researcher found many women say if they had it to do again, they would pick a husband who had the ability to communicate.

Now we don't want men who are reading this to close the book, for many women fall in this category as well. And, if it's any consolation, it takes two to communicate. If there is a problem, both partners need to work together to solve it.

Real communication—the art of talking with each other, saying what we feel, saying it clearly, listening to what the other says, and making sure that we are hearing accurately—is by all indications the skill most essential for creating and maintaining intimate relationships.[1] Not only is communication important to enhance intimacy, but lack of communication can destroy the most intimate relationship.

Communication problems are not new. Do you know the origin of the phrase "bring home the bacon"? In Dunmow, England, there was a tradition that every year a side of bacon would be given to the man who could kneel at the door of the village church and swear that for a year and a day, he and his wife had not quarreled, and at no time did he wish himself unmarried. It was said that between 1244 and 1722 (almost 500 years), the bacon was only awarded eight times!

Even for a side of bacon, it is tough to communicate. And we know personally that you don't have to look at magazine surveys to realize that. Good communication can *make* and bad communication can *break* marriage and family relationships.

Exploration:

What does it take for a spouse to be a great communicator in a Christian marriage?
Write down three attributes you feel are necessary for communication in marriage:

His:

1. _____

2. _____

3. _____

Hers:

1. _____

2. _____

3. _____

The following statements summarize answers given by a group of men and women when we asked them what makes a great communicator. Interestingly, most participants responded alike regardless of gender.

The person is approachable. You can talk to your mate without hesitation or fear. The person is not intimidating.

The person shows genuine concern. Your mate is never too busy or preoccupied but can give you undivided attention when something is on your mind.

The person is open-minded. You can express yourself with your mate and speak in a manner he or she can understand.

The person does not blame the other. Blaming others for our misfortunes is a "primitive mind-set" that goes back to childhood. Many adults have grown up believing that everyone else is responsible for their discomfort. Discomfort is a part of living. We need to assume responsibility for our own lives at some point and learn to cope with difficulties in daily living.[2]

The person exhibits concern by her mannerism and tone of voice. Instead of communicating in anger and harshness, your mate speaks in a manner that is nonthreatening. Words have the power to lift someone up or tear them down, depending on how they are used.

The person acts responsibly. Your mate is respected by all those around him and speaks in a manner that is reverent.

The person fights fair. This means that when there are arguments (and most good marriages have some or someone is getting stomped on!), the person does not fuel the fire with insults, past history, name-calling, and so on.

The person does not keep score. Good communicators compromise equally and don't feel the need to keep a tally on who is giving the most. What does *not* happen in good marriages is scorekeeping, such as "I raise the children," or "I earn the most money."

The person is "safe." Emotional safety is necessary in an intimate marriage. It is the one quality upon which all the other qualities we desire in a relationship—intimacy, openness, and passion—depend. Without emotional safety, a marriage simply will not feel good. When we believe that we are threatened, we defend ourselves; and once defensiveness enters the picture, the possibility of openness and intimacy is lost.[3]

The person does not hold a grudge. Clinging to a grudge is counterproductive. It keeps us from dealing with the problem that initially led us to hold the grudge, and resentment breeds discontent.

The person forgives and forgets. Perhaps this one was crucial among all respondents, that not only did the partner forgive the other for a wrongdoing, but he or she also was willing to forget the incident and move on in a positive manner.

How did your list compare with the list we received? As

much as we would like, not many of us can have these qualities every day. In our marriage, we feel that our communication is strong, yet there are times when one of us might seem more attentive than the other, depending on many factors, such as an exhausting day at work, demanding children, or just not feeling well.

But no matter how deficient we are in our communication skills, in order to become emotionally bonded so that life's interruptions don't wound us permanently, we all can and must work on our communication skills. We can make special efforts to remove stumbling blocks from our past and move on to greater understanding and love.

Discussion or Sparring Session?

The purpose of communication is to understand each others' expectations, needs, feelings, and interests. Developing effective communication skills can enhance intimate marriages and help stabilize rocky ones. They can mean the difference between a lasting, quality relationship and a lifeless marriage or even divorce.

Unfortunately, we all will experience situations that test our relationships, such as loss of employment, death of a parent, loss of a child, or illness in a spouse. Whether we are facing a temporary crisis, or an ongoing, chronic problem beyond our control, poor communication will add to our burdens, inevitably leading to a lack of intimacy, an unhappy marriage, and possibly divorce.

Exploration:

What communication threats occur in your marriage, if any? (criticism, defensiveness, contempt, refusal to cooperate)

Are you willing to change the way you communicate to eliminate these threats?

How would the following describe your communication skills?

- God
- Your partner
- Your children
- Your co-workers
- Your pastor
- Your friends

What do you need to deal with in order to communicate openly and lovingly?

Steps to Breaking the Ice With Communication

Let's face it. We are all very different animals. A marriage can either be a circus in which the animals work together for the common good, a place where bears and lions learn to dance together; or it can be a jungle, where the rule is the survival of the fittest and every animal is out for himself. Verbal sparring sessions will block any hope of increasing the emotional intimacy in your marriage. These are definitely communication techniques to avoid. There is a better way.

Remind yourself that to succeed at communication, you have to recognize and admit that there is a problem—no one is perfect. Once you have identified the areas you are weak in, the next step is to take appropriate action to defuse anger and negative thinking and become more accepting of each other—no matter what kind of baggage you have brought into the relationship.

Use these steps to begin your cease-fire—as you start to break the ice with open and affirming communication.

Step 1: *Start with affirmation.*

Affirm your unity and love. There have been many times in counseling couples when we have said, "Before you tell us what's wrong with your marriage, let's affirm the things that are right with it. Why did you get married in the first place? What are the things that bind you together?"

The tragedy is that after being married for years, we begin to take each other for granted. "He never tells me that he loves me," Charlotte told us about her husband of fifteen years. "I mean, he's a great guy, but I want to hear him say this to me."

Being a great guy can go a long way in having buddies, but to reclaim intimacy in marriage, love must be affirmed. When we begin to take things for granted in the relationship, we lay the groundwork for a breakdown of communication.

One psychologist said, "Bad marriages don't just happen one day with an unsolvable argument. The best predictor of a sour marriage is when men and women allow their love to be unaffirmed, for this love will die."

Affirm your differences. Paul teaches in Ephesians that Christ has given all of us special abilities—whatever he wants us to have out of his rich storehouse of gifts. Yes, even in the best marriages there is diversity. With all this diversity, there is one great purpose: to build up each other in love, to bring each other to maturity, reaching the very height of Christ's full stature.

The amazing affirmation that the apostle Paul makes is that all of these differences are given to help us build each other up and to grow in love. It is when men and women push and tug against each other that they begin to discover who they are and start to mature in love.

Perhaps one of the gravest problems in a marriage is when both partners avoid talking about their differences. They grit their teeth, compromise, avoid, and eventually concede to the other, simply because they do not want to "cause a scene." Yet, in order to affirm our differences, we will need to openly discuss them from time to time—and accept the fact that we don't think alike on every issue. Healthy communication does not mean that you sing in perfect harmony day in and day out. Rather, it means that thoughts and feelings are being dealt with in a respectful manner so that neither party is getting stepped on.

Affirm honesty. As Christians, we know that we are to speak the truth in love. This means that we are to speak plainly and clearly with one another; to be able to say,

- I am angry.
- I feel hurt.
- I feel so alone.
- I am disappointed.
- I feel unloved.

But in the midst of expressing our personal feelings honestly, we must also use tact. As we said before, tact is that delicate perception of knowing the right thing to say or do without offending the other person. (Notice that in the above statements, we have used "I" in each case, not "You make me . . ." Being honest but tactful involves accepting full responsibility for our own feelings without blaming our partner for "making" us feel that way.)

In our marriage, we have experienced that honesty can be very tricky. If you are too honest, your spouse may accuse you of being rude, blunt, and inconsiderate. Yet when you hide your real feelings and tell your partner only what you think he wants to hear, you may come across as phony and insincere. We have experienced that just as we acquired words for goodness, hope, optimism, joy, and love, we have also learned to attach negative symbols and discovered early the power of directing them where we please. Yes, words can hurt.[4]

Just how honest can we be? Should we constantly confront our marriage partners with the whole truth, as painful as it may be, or must we temper our honest communication to avoid hurting those we love most? Here are some techniques that will help you communicate honestly without unnecessarily offending or blaming your spouse:

Choose your words carefully. As you learn to speak the truth without hurting your spouse, learn to reframe the *way* you speak as well, using these techniques:

- Avoid insults, but be very specific as to what the problem is.
- Avoid using hopeless talk, such as "this always happens."
- State the actual problem; don't throw blame.
- Don't label your spouse, such as "lazy," "sloppy," or "selfish."
- Never use absolutes, such as "you always . . ." or "you never . . ."

Focus on confession. We have found confession very important in maintaining a truthful marriage relationship. This means that, if needed, we can temper truthful statements that might be hurtful to our partner if we openly confess our own faults or shortcomings. This vulnerable honesty helps to create an atmosphere of warmth and acceptance between us as we assure our partner that, "Hey, I've been there, too."

When counseling a young couple several months ago, the young man told of being irritable and complained of being tired all the time after he began his new job as a computer salesman. Instead of being upset about his moodiness, his wife was able to offer some helpful advice as she confessed to similar problems.

"I knew just what Stan was going through because I experienced the same thing last year after I began my job at the university," Kate told us. Instead of being angry with him for his bad temper, she shared with him what she had learned in her own stressful work situation. She was able to give him some practical ideas of how to get in control of his life, offering some tips on stress management he could use to function more effectively on the job. Stan was relieved to know that Kate had felt similar pressures and had also found it difficult to control her temper when she was so tired out by her job. Kate's willingness to confess her own shortcomings helped her husband reach a more mature understanding of his limitations, as well as those of his wife. Rather than being pushed apart by mutual anger and frustration, Kate and Stan grew toward a more intimate marriage relationship.

If you can let the other person know that you are with him in the situation being discussed, the chances are greater that healing can take place. Even if you do not have any specific advice as Kate did, just "being there" with your partner can open the door to finding solutions together. It is best to be honest about a problem that exists and not hide your feelings of anger, but do so without tearing down the relationship. Find ways to open the door to solving the problem together.

Show empathy to the other. Empathy is also important in developing honest communication in a marriage and affirming your love for each other. To have empathy means to identify with the feelings and needs of another, to show understanding of their situation—to put yourself in that person's shoes. In our previous example, Kate was not only confessing, but she was also showing *empathy* toward her husband by being sensitive to his needs in a difficult situation. In the Gospels, Jesus teaches us a lifestyle that is full of empathy, of being sensitive to those around us and trying to understand what it would be like to be in their place. This agape or selfless love enables us to meet the personal needs of our spouse, rather than tearing him down.

Compassion, sincerity, and empathy communicate your feelings of friendship and support. We work at having empathy for the other and try to always think before speaking:

- How would I like to hear this message?
- How would it feel hearing these words?
- Would it enable me to grow as a person?
- How could the words be said to promote growth in our relationship?

Messages given in a caring setting are more likely to be taken and acted upon. Again, if you know what your spouse's Achilles' heel is—leave it alone!

Ask, Will this help our marriage to grow? As you affirm honesty in your marriage, it is also important to only tell truths that will help the marriage or the other person grow. We have found that positive truths spoken in love enhance our friendship. But when we share negative opinions critically and thoughtlessly, we only destroy the communication between us.

Step 2: *Avoid keeping score.*

Probably one of the most childish symptoms of poor communication lies in that person who keeps score. Jeanne told of keeping track of how many times Dan came home late from work. "When he came home an hour late five times in a two-month period, I decided to get even," she said. "So I took the kids and we went out to dinner and to a movie. You should have seen his face when we got home after 10:00 P.M. Dan had been worried sick for hours."

Did Jeanne's game plan work with Dan? No, he continued to come home from work late periodically, especially when traffic tie-ups delayed him. But what keeping score did for Jeanne was help to further disrupt the harmony in their marriage. She was always ready to show Dan that she had "one up on him" and carried a grudge for years that prevented them from addressing intimate issues.

Preoccupation with how badly you've been treated in years past causes a tremendous amount of distracting mental activity that keeps us from communicating productively. It's extraordinary how much time men and women spend plotting revenge, worrying themselves sick about being cheated, and feeling angry or sad—all emotions and thoughts that interfere with reaching the goal of intimacy in marriage.[5]

As you continue your Intimate Journey this week, think of all the past history about your marriage that you need to let go of. Realize that keeping a grudge will get you nowhere when it comes to emotional intimacy; it will only add fuel to the fire and cause resentment from your spouse. Throw away all un-written grudges that you have on your heart to experience a satisfying and compromising marriage.

Step 3: *Watch labeling your spouse.*

We must be honest and say that in our marriage, there have been impulsive moments when we have carelessly labeled each other. Deb has said to Bob, "You are always so jumpy," and Bob, in turn, has quipped that Deb is "always so cluttered." As insignificant as these labels may seem, nicknames can be dev-astating for any person, especially when tagged with the word "always." How can we ever break free of that?

Labels are usually developed out of the habit of continually emphasizing only one dominant trait in a person. And while the label may sometimes be positive, the remark is usually de-rogatory.

We believe that one of the greatest hazards in labeling your spouse is that it limits the person's God-given potential. A wife who is labeled as "a carefree spendthrift" may try to live up to her name. While the husband who is called "irresponsible" may merely accept this about himself. In marriage, our ideas and perceptions of our mates should change as each of us grows and matures. Often we keep a fixed opinion of what a person is like and then never allow for change or growth.

Now we must qualify that labeling is not the same as having a pet name for your partner. Nicknames or pet names are even healthy for a relationship as they are usually a celebration of your love together.

Encouragement is important as you let your mate reach his or her fullest potential, and as you help him build inner strengths. This encouragement means avoiding comparing your husband or wife with someone else and accepting that

person's uniqueness, realizing that God made us to complement one another.

Step 4: *Learn to listen.*

Isn't it amazing how well we listen to a good friend when
we are interested in the subject? Yet, what happens when the
discussion is between husband and wife? Often we tune out
the conversation, ignore our spouse, and use all sorts of body
language to let the other person feel that we are not interested
in his thoughts or opinion.

But did you know that your reaction to your spouse's words
determines how much he or she will communicate with you?
If you come across as unyielding, then your spouse may feel
that it is worthless talking with you and may quit talking altogether. Yet, if you listen to the other person's reasoning, try
to relate to what he is saying without judging what is being
said, and then give replies that are fair and reasonable, you are
opening the door to loving communication in your marriage.

Being an effective listener is vital in breaking the ice in
communication and in establishing a more intimate relationship. When feelings and thoughts are poured out and real listening occurs, your spouse will feel loved and understood. Our
own Lord exhibited these same listening skills as he patiently
dealt with people and problems each day. In fact, the Bible has
much to teach about communication. Remember in John 8:
1–11 how Jesus patiently listened to the scribes and Pharisees
as they accused the woman of adultery, his kind words to her,
and how he solved the problem without harsh punishment?
Yes, Jesus listened intently to the problem before reacting in
love.

Look directly at your spouse when talking. While listening, refuse to talk to or look at anyone else, even if just to smile. Each
time you look away while listening to your spouse, the trend
of thought is diminished. And each time you pay attention, you
are showing courtesy to someone you love.

Make sure that you understand what is being said. Ask your spouse questions about the subject being discussed. Do not assume anything that is not said without questioning the topic. Replay what your spouse says and ask if it is correct, such as "Did I hear you say that. . . ?" Get all of the facts straight before offering an opinion, a suggestion, or a comment.

Force yourself to keep your mind on the subject being discussed. Don't let your mind wander to the problems at work or needs of the home. Instead, try to identify with your spouse and what he is telling you. Reflect on your own life. Were you ever in a situation where someone did not listen to you when you were talking to them? How did it feel? How did you deal with it? Think and respond as your spouse pours out his thoughts and feelings.

Care enough to be sensitive about what is being said, even if it is totally irrelevant to your life. Don't shrug off your spouse's words and feelings. Rather, empathize with him. Compassion, sincerity, and empathy communicate your feelings of friendship and support. A relationship that really works and involves personal caring means going that extra mile—together!

Accept what your spouse is telling you. This does not mean that you have to agree with his view or opinion, but simply accept what he is saying as valid. This unconditional acceptance relays a caring message as you respect his feelings.

Watch your body language. In a marriage, you will use all sorts of signs, symbols, smiles, and other gestures to express caring and love, as well as distrust, disgust, and anger, for communication doesn't mean just talking or listening; it includes all the clues to a person's feelings. An inappropriate smile can be just as negative or even more so than not smiling at all during a heated discussion with your spouse.

While body language occurs unconsciously, it makes up 90 percent of effective communication. The way you sit or stand, the way you cross your legs, and the way you gesture or smile while you listen greatly affects how the other person feels. If your posture is poor and how you reply to the other person is equally offensive, your partner will feel that you're not really listening to them. Good listening skills require body language that tells your partner you are tuned in and really hearing what they're saying without forming judgments.

Facial expressions are an important part of your body language and will enhance or detract from your listening skills. An affable, responsive face can be a tremendous asset when communicating with your spouse. Your expressions can share confidence and conviction as your partner confides in you with openness. And if you make eye contact and keep it, your eyes will pick up how the person is responding to what you say.

Listening skills are vital not only in making people feel loved and affirmed, but also in letting them feel understood. If you come across as uninterested when your spouse communicates honestly with you, he may feel that it is worthless talking with you and quit talking altogether. Yet, if you REALLY listen to him, you can have empathy for his situation in life.

Step 5: *Realize that conflict is inevitable.*

If you have no fights in an intimate relationship, then something is wrong. Relationships are about give-and-take, and we all must express ourselves in order for this to happen. The first conflict in the human family is recorded in the Bible in Genesis 3:12—Adam's criticism of Eve. A family feud in God's Word? Yes, and there are many family feuds in the finest Christian homes today.

Many people resent conflict in the home. "I wish it would just go away," Amy told us. "As soon as I think we might have an argument, I clam up inside and want to run."

Conflict may be defined as a sharp disagreement or opposition, as of interests, ideas, and so forth. Even the most vibrant and caring Christian families experience this from time to time.

Many of the conflicts between men and women arise from age-old differences. Pretending that these differences don't exist builds misunderstanding, frustration, and distrust. But when we accept that the sexes are coming from "different directions," with different goals, we can begin to understand each other better.[6]

The conflict we all experience in our marriages is nothing new. We can look in the Bible and see that even in the earliest days of the Church, people experienced the difficulty of facing conflict and resolving this to find a peaceful solution. Yet Paul affirmed the unity of Christians (even though different in many ways) in Romans 12:5: "So we, though many, are one body in Christ" (RSV).

Dr. Richard Dobbins suggests an excellent three-stage process for using conflict to build unity in the home:

1. *Desensitization.* Tell the other your feelings using "I" statements instead of blaming with "you" statements. Take responsibility for your own feelings instead of pouting or blowing up to control the other. Learn to tolerate the tension of expressed differences. Otherwise, they go underground and can do even more damage. Listen without defensiveness to the other's feelings.

2. *Deliberation.* "Do not let the sun go down on your anger" (Ephesians 4:26, RSV). Discuss the options for settling the problem. Negotiate the pros and cons of each choice. Neither party is allowed to rule by denial or domination.

3. *Decision.* Settle on an option and pursue it. Monitor the progress of the agreement. All parties are accountable to the decision. Stay on the subject, and have your discussions in private. Whatever you do, do not walk out while seeking unity.[7]

When you have conflict, listen to each other, using the principles in Step 4: *Learn to listen,* and actually hear the other's point of view. Realize that there does not have to be a winner or loser. Step back and let go of some of the control while preserving your relationship.

Step 6: *Temper your anger.*

Some people, when they are angry, "let it all hang out" in their relationships with others. They thrive on this emotion and blow up in every direction. They scream at family members, kick the dog, hang up on co-workers, or put fists through walls. "I'm so sorry," they may say after the damage is done. Often these men and women excuse themselves, saying they have an uncontrollable temper. You must know that there is no such thing as an uncontrollable temper. We are all able to maintain control over our anger and the way we express it.

"But my temper goes quickly," you may argue. "It's over within seconds, and I feel better ventilating my anger." A shotgun blast is also over within seconds, but it blows everything to bits.

You must first understand that anger is a universal human phenomenon. It is a normal reaction to life situations, and how one reacts to the anger can vary from one person to another. The problem arises when anger consumes our whole being or is displayed in hurtful and inappropriate ways.

Anger comes from a hostile personality fight-or-flight response. This inborn response—as old as mankind itself—primes the body to respond to physical threats. The heart boosts its output from four or five quarts of blood a minute to eighteen to twenty quarts . . . the adrenal glands release adrenaline and other powerful hormones . . . and the thinking becomes highly focused.[8]

Exploration:

How do you express anger toward your spouse?
- yelling
- turning inward
- crying
- eating
- avoiding arguments

Understanding Anger

From emotions such as hurt, fear, guilt, jealousy, or dis-appointment comes anger. To cope with the anger that often accompanies relationships, it is important to understand the types of anger we can feel.

Upfront anger is expressed directly toward the person or situation at which the person is angry. This type of anger, if not overemphasized, is most acceptable as the person expresses feelings to the one involved. Statements such as "that charge card bill really made me mad." Or, "I feel so angry inside when your father tries to come between us," are acceptable IF you do not follow through with violent outbursts.

Displaced anger originates from strong feelings toward a person or event, but is directed toward a different person or event. For example, your partner may fuss at you and suggest that "you are ignoring the children while watching too many sports events at night." Instead of expressing your anger toward her for the comment, you scream at your son when he walks in front of the television screen, expressing displaced anger. This anger carries the most painful result because innocent victims are the object of your loss of control.

Inward anger is unexpressed, either verbally or nonverbally.

Instead of speaking openly about your angry thoughts, you may let them boil up inside and eat away at your entire being, resulting in physical ailments such as nausea, tension headaches, muscle aches, hypertension, or even depression.

It is so easy to be stopped by anger, frustration, or disappointment. But we can move forward by reminding ourselves that love is not just something we feel or something we get. Love is an active word; it is something we do!

The Bible has much to teach us about anger and about self-control as even Christ Jesus became angry in the synagogue. The marketing of wares in God's house on the Sabbath, at inflated prices, no less, was against the principles he held close to his heart. Paul speaks of self-control during times of anger, saying, "But when the Holy Spirit controls our lives he will produce this kind of fruit in us: love, joy, peace, patience, kindness, goodness, faithfulness, gentleness and self-control" (Galatians 5:22–23).

In Ephesians 4:31–32 we read: "Stop being mean, bad-tempered and angry. Quarreling, harsh words, and dislike of others should have no place in your lives. Instead, be kind to each other, tenderhearted, forgiving one another, just as God has forgiven you because you belong to Christ." What does it mean to get rid of our anger, and how can this be done without hurting the very ones we love?

First, we must learn to express our anger constructively. This means without swearing, hitting, yelling, or injuring those innocent "victims" around us. If we cannot express our anger constructively, the Christian way of dealing with it is to go to the person who has offended us or incited our anger and try to square accounts.

Talk with your spouse about the problems of anger that is not expressed in a positive manner. Anger can destroy her health as well as your relationship. One study tested couples for their reaction to an argument. It found that the higher their hostility, the higher their blood pressure rate. The hormones regulating the immune system changed as well, affecting their ability to fight disease.[9]

Communication is the key to resolving angry feelings, but you must also find the best moment to do this. Being direct and honest about the problem without being condescending is the best way to smooth harsh feelings.

The goal of learning to deal with anger in an acceptable manner is to move from anger to reconciliation. If you and your partner are in the midst of a heated argument because of one's anger, immediately allow space between you. This will let the storm reside, until you both can come back and look at the anger as being very real, but also very detrimental to health and an intimate relationship. Sometimes our best service to those we love is to simply stand by, be silent, be patient, be hopeful, be understanding, and wait.[10]

As you and your spouse accept each other's feelings as being very real, remain sensitive to the views of each other, and channel your anger in creative and appropriate ways, you both can experience reconciliation. If reconciliation does not work, and sometimes it doesn't, then turn the situation over to God. Pray, "Lord, I've done all I can. Whatever happens, please take the ache of anger and resentment out of my heart before it becomes destructive to me and to others." Can you think of a better alternative to ending unreconciled anger? We think not.

If you or your spouse are unable to control anger, and it is consuming your life, seek the help of your pastor or physician. Ask for a recommendation of a professional who can give you some tools for coping with angry feelings.

Week Three: Cease Fire! Break the Ice With Communication

Focus: More important than relearning how to communicate is to create an environment in your marriage where you can share love and warm conversation with each other.

A major barrier to good communication is the lack of time that couples have together. This is especially true for the two-career couples and couples with children. Sometimes it is easier to forget all the things you like about each other than it is to work toward a creative solution to finding more time in your schedule to be together.

This week make an effort to spend time alone together—preferably when you are not exhausted. Take the phone off the hook; put the kids to bed early; plan one evening a week with no chores; ship the kids off to Grandma's for the weekend; set aside one evening a month for dinner or a movie together; and relax.[11]

We want you to focus on seven ways to increase emotional intimacy in your relationship. After reading this chapter, use the following actions to work through communication gaps in your marriage.

Central Bible Truth: "Don't ever forget that it is best to listen much, speak little, and not become angry; for anger doesn't make us good, as God demands that we must be" (James 1:19–20).

Monday: *Focus on saying thanks.*

You can talk honestly and lovingly without mentioning the word love. Think about it. How many times do you say thank you to a co-worker? To a close friend? To the clerk at the grocery store? Yet, how many times do we avoid saying thank you to the one we love most—our spouse? Politeness and saying thanks creates a solid foundation for intimacy in marriage, yet studies show that people who are the least polite to each other are married couples.

Reflection and response:

Watch for times today where you can interject the words "thank you" in conversation with your spouse. Have you ever used these before? Write down how you feel about not taking your spouse for granted and becoming more appreciative. Make these words part of your vocabulary.

His: _____

_____

Hers: _____

_____

Tuesday: *Listen and really hear your spouse.*

Communication, the art of talking with each other, saying what we feel and mean, saying it clearly, listening to what the other says, and making sure that we're hearing accurately, is by all indication the skill most essential for creating and maintaining loving relationships.[12]

Make an effort today to listen to your spouse and really hear what she is saying. Sometimes the best reaction you can give to someone's conversation is to patiently listen and show that you are with them.

Reflection and response:

Write down a time today when you noticed yourself becoming distracted while your spouse was speaking. What was getting your attention? Try to make a more conscious effort to tune in and really hear what your spouse is saying.

His: _____

_____

Hers: _____

_____

Wednesday: *Try the Five-to-One Rule.*

Make it a point today to compliment your spouse, and mean it! Studies have shown that in intimate marriages, the ratio of positives to negatives is approximately five to one. Make sure as you begin on this Intimate Journey with your spouse that your ratio becomes at least five to one.

Example:

Positives	Negatives
compliments	criticism
being helpful	ignoring
showing compassion	showing negative feelings
hugs and kisses	anger and bitterness
empathy	nagging

Reflection and response:

His: _____

_____

Hers: _____

_____

Thursday: *Relearn trust.*

Being who we are requires that we can talk openly about things that are important to us, that we take a clear position on where we stand on important emotional issues, and that we clarify the limits of what is acceptable and what is tolerable to us in a relationship. Allowing the other person to do the same means we can stay emotionally connected with that other party who thinks, feels, and believes differently, without needing to change, convince, or fix the other.[13]

Harboring grudges or negative thoughts about your spouse is detrimental to your health and your relationship. With an open mind and heart, ask God for help you to regain trust in your marriage.

Reflection and response:

Because grudges can involve such powerful feelings, use this time to get rid of—forever—any negative thoughts or past history that you have been clinging to about your spouse. This will not be easy, but in order to relearn the trust and intimate feelings that you once had, you must put aside resentments.

Write down your grudge(s) and resentment(s)—along with all your feelings about them—on a piece of paper and literally bury them in the backyard. As you do this, bury any negative feelings that went with the grudge. Make a commitment to yourself not to think about this grudge for the rest of the Intimate Journey—do not bring it up to your spouse and do not harbor it with compulsive worry.

Write down your feelings of freedom for getting rid of resentments you might have had.

His: _____

_____

Hers: _____

_____

Friday: *Express anger appropriately.*

Anger is an emotion that can destroy your health and your relationship, if not expressed in a positive manner. Anger is also an emotion that everyone is entitled to feel at times, but again, it is important to express this in a way that will not be detrimental to your overall health and well-being, or to those around you. It is so easy to be stopped by anger, frustration, or disappointment. We move forward by reminding ourselves that love is not just something we feel or something we get. Love is something we do.[14]

Reflection and response:

Remember that love enhances a relationship, it does not degrade it. Love builds the self-esteem of our partner. It does not diminish it. Put-downs that attempt to change someone's behavior usually tend to aggravate it.[15] If anger is consuming your entire day, realize that you need to find some areas for changing this. Sit down with your partner and take an inventory of how anger is affecting your relationship. Then using the blanks on this page, write down the very situations that create angry feelings in you. It is important to accept responsibility for your anger; do not place the blame on your spouse. Instead, write down the situation. Then in the corresponding blank, write down creative ways to solve the problems.

Sample:

Anger situation: I get angry when dinner is late each night after working all day.
Creative solution: Let's plan ahead the night before so we both can help prepare dinner.

Anger situation: I get angry when my clients say our phone line is busy all day.
Creative solution: Let's look into getting Call Waiting from the phone company, and let's also use an egg timer to limit our phone calls.

His:

Anger situation: _____

_____

Creative solution: _____

_____

Anger situation: _____

_____

Creative solution: _____

_____

Hers:

Anger situation: _____

_____

Creative solution: _____

_____

Anger situation: _____

_____

Creative solution: _____

_____

Saturday: *Communicate friendship through touch.*

A pat on the shoulder, a warm hug, or a tender kiss on the cheek often generates a strong sense of caring and concern which is important for a best friendship in a marriage. In a recent study at a large northern university, a number of students who checked out books at the university library were given a handshake, a pat on the arm, or other touch by staff librarians. After leaving the building, each student was questioned about his feelings about the school's library. Of the students who had been touched, one hundred percent reported positive feelings. But those who were not touched had either apathetic or negative feelings.

Use this nonverbal and nonsexual form of caring with your spouse at least five times today. Your touch may be the security she longs for.

Reflection and response:

His: _____

_____

Hers: _____

_____

Sunday: *Communicate compassion in your marriage.*

Compassion is the ability to feel with another person. We need to take a second look at our spouse and our children and ask ourselves, "Do I have any understanding of the experiences that have brought him or her to this place in life? Is there anything I can do to make his life or her life easier and more meaningful?"

Reflection and response:

As you review week three of your Intimate Journey, write down two new insights you've gained about yourself and about your spouse in how you communicate with each other. Use this knowledge to improve your intimate communication skills.

His:

About me:

1. _____

2. _____

About you:

1. _____

2. _____

Hers:

About me:

1. _____

2. _____

About you:

1. _____

2. _____

4

WEEK FOUR
Make Time for Romance

For centuries couples have experienced the spectacular oneness felt in the physical union of marriage. To lie close in your partner's arms within marriage exudes feelings of warmth, confidence, and protection. The emotional act of loving each other also solidifies the self-giving of the marriage commitment and brings two separate individuals together in a way that makes them as one—two distinct souls passionately meshing into one new and complete being.

What about those relationships where marital partners don't experience physical closeness? Some say it is normal for a marriage relationship to become comfortable with this situation as partners become busy with children, careers, and personal interests. While this may get the job done, daily distractions and responsibilities also pull us apart emotionally. However, we have experienced that the longer a marriage goes feeling too content without sex, the more difficult it is to pull it off the back burner when adversity hits or major life changes occur, when you need to be intimately bonded.

As Stanley explained, "For twenty-five years, Janet took care of the kids and I worked outside the home. But when our youngest child left for college, we were so out of touch with each other's daily realities that we didn't feel sexually attracted to each other and had to relearn how to be physically intimate."

What comes between you and your partner as far as sex is concerned? If you think about it for a minute, we're sure you will come up with a list similar to this:

- She's too worried about neatness.
- He makes his business more important than our relationship.
- She is such a perfectionist that I feel uncomfortable.
- He's a workaholic and has no time for sexual relations.
- She doesn't understand what I go through each day and why I'm too tired for sex.
- He listens, but does not really hear what I am saying.
- She's always too tired or distracted when I get home from work.
- He would rather watch sports on TV than be intimate with me.
- Since she started working, she's too exhausted to even fix dinner for the family, much less think about sex.

And the list goes on. In studies taken on failed marriages, sexual incompatibility was the third most common marital problem. This goes hand-in-hand with poor communication—if you can't talk to each other, the intimacy in a marriage is stilted as well.

There is little question that personal dissatisfaction with sex within marriage is commonplace in our society today. In fact, some studies reveal that half of all American marriages are troubled by some form of sexual distress ranging from disinterest and boredom to outright sexual dysfunction. The sexual problems people tell about most frequently have to do with inhibitions and guilt, performance anxiety, erotic boredom, and blind acceptance of sexual misinformation or myths. In fact, these four problems collectively account for more than 80 percent of the sexual dissatisfactions in modern America.[1]

Why Sex Is Important for Intimacy

Even though we qualify intimacy as emotional connectedness, sexual satisfaction is necessary to reclaim this in your marriage. Why is sex important?

Sex in marriage is part of God's plan for men and women. When God created sexuality, he called it very good. In that regard, our heavenly Father views sex within marriage as pure and having spiritual meaning. (Read Ephesians 5:30–32.) God promises that when two people are united sexually, the two will become one flesh. This means the blending of two very different personalities into one new creation.

Sex is physically satisfying. We all need to be touched and held and to release sexual tensions that build up inside of us.

Having sex with someone we love creates more intimacy and closeness between us. Having sex with our husband or wife, especially when we are making love and not just having sex, makes us feel special, valued, and cared for.

A healthy sex life builds our self-esteem. When we feel we are good lovers and are desired by another, our sense of self-worth increases.[2]

Sex is the emotional barometer of a marriage. If there are problems in any area of the relationship—financial, communication, parenting—these will show up in the sex life.

Sex is a healthy part of life. Sex triggers the release of endorphins, chemicals that make us feel positive and happy. Studies show that these endorphins released during lovemaking work like a tranquilizer on the body, helping to soothe and relax you.

Exploration:

- What stumbling blocks do you have in your sexual relationship? (no time, children always around, too tired, other)
- How would you rate your sexual relationship? Is it fulfilling, adequate, or needs some energy?
- What changes need to happen before you can experience intimacy within your sexual relationship? (priorities need changing, need time alone together, need to put work aside, need to focus on each other's needs, other)

Role Mates or Soulmates?

Do you remember the beginning of your dating relationship? You were so madly in love and so close. "It's as if I knew him all my life after just three dates," one middle-aged woman said.

So what happened to the passion, to the fervor you felt toward each other? How can you re-ignite flames of intimacy in your marriage? According to Florida-based marriage and family counselor Allan Decker, men and women start out wanting to be close and to get along with one another. "The problem is that we come to our partners with fully packed bags," Decker contends. "This baggage is stuffed with the stories and teachings of our family of origin."

Decker claims that the way one family socializes its members may be totally different from your partner's experience. Both partners may say they understand, but their deeply ingrained teachings socialize them to try to get their own way. Also, all relationships are an attempt to make things right and to fulfill the wishes that were left unfulfilled from the families we grew up in. We expect our wives and husbands to complete our unfinished longings.

Many people grew up in traditional families where fathers were the financial providers and mothers were the emotional providers. In this type of family, the husband and wife are said to be Role Mates. In contrast, the men and women of the nineties are attempting to be Soulmates.[3] This difference is best described in Warren Farrell's book *The Myth of Male Power*, in which he talks about Stage I and Stage II marriages or relationships.[4]

Stage I Marriage: For thousands of years most marriages were Stage I. They were survival-focused marriages and promoted separateness between men and women. Couples were Role Mates. The woman raised the children; the man raised the money. A woman called it "love" if she found a man who was a good provider and protector. Likewise, a man called it "love" if the woman was beautiful and could take care of the home and raise the children. The term "love" actually meant a division of labor. This meant a division of female and male interests.

Stage II Marriage: Stage II marriages are self-fulfillment focused. Couples redefine love by becoming Soulmates. In this type of relationship, "love" means blending common interests and common values. The woman who married the most successful man had the most freedom and time to redefine love. Perhaps she pondered Stage II questions like, "Should I settle for a man who will show me his wallet when I'd rather see his love, attention, and affection?"

What defines a Stage II marriage? Couples expect:

- communication skills
- joint parenting
- shared housework
- sexual fulfillment
- joint decision-making

- mutual respect

Stage II marriages are built on both stability and change, both independence and interdependence. Couples want time to grow and discover each other's growth. These needs would have directly threatened the survival of Stage I couples. It would have taken away from raising the children, raising the crops, and raising money.

The problem is that when people marry someone who will fulfill their Stage I needs, that person may fall short of satisfying the Stage II desires. A woman marries a lawyer, a doctor, or a businessman who is a terrific financial provider. He is a good provider because he is competitive, resourceful, and driven in his work. The woman also expects him to be sensitive, compassionate, and caring. He is expected to suppress the attributes that make him a good provider and substitute those of a poet, a writer, or a person who may be more creative but less likely to provide well.

He marries a woman who is beautiful and takes good care of the house and kids. Does he marry a career woman who is independent, wants to work outside the home, and prefers that others raise their kids? In both these cases, we see that the qualities that are needed for the Stage I/Traditional Couple are not the same traits you would want for the Stage II, Nineties Couple.

Sex Is Viewed Differently by Men and Women

No matter if you rate your relationship a Stage I marriage or Stage II, it is important to first understand that sex is viewed differently by the sexes. For most men, being sexual is a way of being intimate. Women usually see sex as a precursor to being intimate. It sounds terribly traditional and old-fashioned, but still it is true: when men feel lonely and hurt, they want to be held and make love. When women feel hurt, they want to be understood and talked to. This difference is very confusing and causes incredible problems between couples.[5]

We have experienced in counseling many couples that both men and women are looking for the same things in a marriage relationship, that is, a sense of connection, intimacy, and love. But, somehow, we often go about meeting these needs in very different ways. Author John Gray says that for most men, the primary way of connecting is through sex. Women connect primarily through verbal communication.

"When a woman feels that her need for communication is not being taken seriously by her partner, she begins to lose her enthusiasm for sex. Similarly, if a man isn't getting his sexual needs satisfied, his ability to be expressive in other ways tends to diminish."

Gray assesses that fortunately the opposite is also true. When a woman's communication needs are met, sex becomes more satisfying to her and she can enjoy it freely. When a man's sexual needs are regularly satisfied, he is more open to verbal sharing.[6]

Are you and your partner sexually compatible? Sex within marriage is part of God's plan. (See Genesis, chapters 1 and 2.) However, if this is so, why do so many couples today tell of being sexually unsatisfied?

Steps to Making Time for Romance

Perhaps what we all need to be reminded of as we work to reclaim intimacy in our marriages is that it requires both time and energy to nurture sexuality between husband and wife. This ultimate form of intimacy is not something you ignore for months, or even years for some people, then suddenly pick up one day when "the mood hits." Rather, physical contact must happen regularly for you to stay intimately bonded. This does not mean that you must make love all the time, but sexual intimacy requires regular physical connectedness—intimate, physical encounters that allow you to bond in body, mind, and spirit.

Step 1: *Make sex a priority in your marriage.*

To reclaim intimacy and closeness, make time on a regular basis to be together—alone.

Step 2: *Rediscover dating.*

Dating allows you to make time to know your spouse—his/her ups-and-downs, inner fears, goals, and dreams. The exciting reward of dating while being married is that once you know your spouse's needs, you can work at fulfilling them.

But making time for dating and placing your spouse's needs in front of your own isn't easy. Before we were married twenty-three years ago, we certainly did not question this constant self-giving. Dating and spending time together was natural, because we had no other commitments or diversions in life. But after being married for many years, this giving is not so simple. In some marriages, stumbling blocks occur, such as jealousy, selfishness, anxieties, and fears, which can be destructive to the marriage relationship.

We experience an intimate and growing relationship in our marriage by making persistent dating efforts—to be together regularly—to listen, to understand, and to be understood. Our close friend Linda tells of having a regularly scheduled Friday night date with her husband, John.

"We have found that one special night together each week when a delicious meal is served, with time for lingering conversation, adds sparks to our marriage," Linda shared. "We have an unwritten agreement that nothing except an emergency can interrupt our time together. With four children, adopting this one certain night for 'date night' has forced us to make time to spend time alone, and it has strengthened our sexual relationship."

Joe told of having to continually work at finding time to be alone with his wife. "Just because the marriage has lasted for many years does not guarantee that the spark of fun and enthusiasm has continued." Joe and Sarah, his wife of fourteen years, have worked to enjoy similar recreational activities—golfing, bowling, and tennis—building their friendship while dating.

Other couples find working together in the same second career a way to realize their goals while they maintain that special "dating" spark. Sharon and Pete began to write fiction for young adults as a joint hobby shared in the evenings. Not only did they enjoy the writing, but they also began to learn more of each other's inner feelings, emotions, and dreams.

Sharon told of finding an "empty nest" when their children moved into the teen years and spent much of their time with friends away from home. "We found that our lives were very empty," Sharon said. "We had filled every available minute with caring for our children for over fifteen years, and had honestly ignored our marriage relationship. Pete and I spent many lonely nights just watching TV. Then we decided it was time to get to know each other again. Through our writing hobby, we have discovered each other once more while having fun."

Developing an intimate relationship while dating involves sacrifice. For some, it may mean a night at the ballet to please one spouse, or sitting on the hard bleachers at a football game in freezing temperatures to please the other. In our marriage, this sacrifice involves Deb watching Sunday afternoon sports without too much grumbling, and Bob going shopping without complaint.

Make time to be together—alone. "But there is no alone time in our home," you might say. As parents of three, we know how difficult it is to find time to be alone together without children around. It becomes even more difficult as our circadian rhythms are opposite—I (Deb) go to bed early; Bob sleeps later. But we believe that these obstacles only serve as a challenge for us to make time to be together.

When our three children were at home, we found all sorts of creative ways for meeting together, from hiring sitters on weekend nights to meeting at a nearby hotel for an overnight honeymoon.

You might try the following:

- Make one night a week "date" night, and have a regular sitter.
- Check into a hotel for one night every few months.
- Check into a hotel for one afternoon periodically.
- Meet for a romantic lunch at home while children are in school or are napping.
- Rent a fun video for the children to keep them entertained.
- Trade children with another couple each Friday and Saturday night, so both couples have one romantic night each week.
- Go to work an hour late periodically, after the children have left for school.
- Hire a sitter on a special weekend night to take the children on a long walk or to a nearby playground, so you can be alone.

Every couple is different; you will need to find what will work for you and your partner. If your partner is not creative, then take the initiative and make romantic plans for both of you. It's never too late.

"How can we find time to be together?" one young couple asked. "With three preschoolers, there is always someone in our bed right between us." It is important to know that feelings of closeness can be recaptured with a bit of forethought. But, again, this means that one partner is going to have to plan for these intimate times together, including lining up sitters, rearranging work schedules, or making reservations at local hotels or restaurants.

Step 3: *Focus on your partner.*

We believe in partner-centered sex, rather than the typical mechanical sex that many marriages experience. What this means is that each of us stays centered on being sensitive to the other person's physical needs throughout the day, whether spoken or unspoken. In doing this, we have found that touch is a very important sense that can increase sexual pleasure when used prior to making love. Those gentle touches, kisses before leaving for work, and warm hugs throughout the day build naturally into a romantic evening.

"The only time we touch each other is when we have sex," Marilyn, a thirty-two-year-old woman, complained. "I just need more than that in my life." What Marilyn wanted more of was not sex, but hugging, kissing, and pats of affection *before* they went into the bedroom.

Many of us are guilty of forgetting how important it is to kiss our partner throughout the day or give a warm hug for no reason at all, when touch may be the key to helping our partner relax, let down his/her guard, and feel loved.

Touch is crucial for life. In the 1950s, psychologist Harry Harlow proved just how vital touch is for all of us, and how devastating a lack of touch can be, in his classic experiment with rhesus monkeys. He separated infant rhesus monkeys from their natural mothers and put them in a cage with two surrogate mothers. One surrogate was a warm, bare-wire tube with a milk bottle attached to it. The other surrogate was an equally warm cylinder covered with terry cloth. Harlow discovered that the baby monkeys clung to the terry-cloth figure even though the bare-wire surrogate had the milk bottle, which provided these monkeys with their only source of food. When they were confronted with a frightening object, they dashed back to the terry-cloth figure, not to the milk-providing one— to seek comfort. Harlow concluded that these monkeys needed the warmth and security of touch as much as, if not more than, food.[7]

A counselor told us, "I was talking with a couple recently. I asked the husband if he felt loved by his wife, and he replied, 'Of course I do.' Then I turned to the young wife and asked the same. Tearfully, she replied, 'No, I don't.' The husband was very surprised with her statement and said, 'Sweetheart, I tell you I love you every day.' But the young woman said sadly, 'You never hug me. . . .' "

Rediscovering touch in your marital relationship is a must as you become more romantic or sexual with your spouse. Dr. Harold Falk at the Menninger Foundation says, "Hugging can lift depression, enabling the body's immune system to become tuned up. Hugging breathes fresh life into tired bodies and makes you feel younger and more vibrant. In the home, hugging can strengthen relationships and significantly reduce tensions."[8]

We don't have to depend on modern science to tell us that touch is important in increasing marital intimacy. In his ministry, Jesus expressed concern and healed many persons through the use of his hands. In the story of Jesus receiving the little children despite his disciples' objections, "he took the children into his arms and placed his hands on their heads and he blessed them" (Mark 10:16). In Matthew 8:14–15, when Peter's mother-in-law was ill, Jesus touched her hands and the fever left her.

We visualize our Lord putting his arms around children, lifting up the lame, and embracing those in pain. As he preached love and concern, he also demonstrated these traits. He reached out with gentle, caring hands, touching cold and empty lives with his power.

We often emphasize sex in marriage when speaking of touch. But a loving touch can enable you to be sensitive to your spouse in situations where words seem out of place. You can do this by offering those extra strokes and hugs even when your partner is not very lovable. A tender pat on the shoulder, a warm hug, a gentle caress, an unexpected kiss, or other sensual strokes usually generate a stronger sense of caring and concern than spoken words. Touching breaks down barriers and says, "I love and care about you."

Especially as life's interruptions become more frequent for you and your partner, the need for physical closeness seems to become most apparent. In fact, it has been said that a simple caress has the potential of changing a whole life. On the other hand, refusing to touch can break an intimate moment or relationship. This warm embrace, withheld at the vital moment when it is most desperately needed, can easily be the act, or rather the non-act, that finally destroys a relationship.[9]

Step 4: *Stay centered on your partner.*

The heightened feelings experienced when making love are totally dependent on being aware of what your partner is feeling, and this can only happen when there is a meeting of the minds between you. Although tenderness seems to be more of a feminine quality, men can learn to be more attuned to what feels good to their mate. Learning how to sensitively touch the skin to make your mate feel loved and wanted can be learned. While tenderness and gentleness are really intuitive, sometimes we have to reach deep and rediscover our natural ability.

To learn greater sensitivity for our partner's needs and move toward a more intimate relationship, we must understand the differences between what men and women need in a relationship.

What men need: Making the transition from a Stage I to a Stage II relationship requires that women become sensitive about a man's need to be trusted, accepted, and appreciated. He especially wants to be appreciated for being a good provider. Supporting his family is one of the ways that a man shows he loves his wife and children. A man is often fearful that someone will try to change him. He defends himself strongly against messages that he is not good enough as he is. His self-esteem is defined by his ability to achieve results and to be supportive and accepted by the people he loves, so that when he is offered unsolicited advice, it sends the message that he is incompetent. Men are trying not to feel embarrassed or shamed. For him life is a struggle to preserve independence and avoid failure.

What women need: Women need love that is caring, under-standing, and respectful. According to author John Gray (*Men Are From Mars, Women Are From Venus*), during a woman's "downtime," she needs to talk and be listened to. This is the time when men do not need to "fix" things. The last thing a woman wants when she is feeling down is someone telling her how to fix things and why she shouldn't be down.

To resolve conflict, be supportive. When couples fight, men argue for the right to be free while women argue for the right to be upset. Men want space, women want understand-ing. To resolve conflicts, a man can support his wife's need to be heard, while a woman can support her husband's need to be free. If a person is not allowed to be unhappy sometimes, then they can never truly be happy. If we want to feel the positive feelings of love, happiness, trust, and gratitude, we need to be able to feel anger, sadness, fear, and sorrow from time to time.[10]

Step 5: *Lean on the little things.*

"So, what's the secret of your romance?" a married couple asked at a recent seminar. In our marriage, we find it natural to be romantic toward each other as we share the load at home. We work daily at making life better for the other person and lean on the little things to strengthen the whole.

Now perhaps that sounds trite, but it truly works in letting the other person know how important he is. This may mean Deb folds the clothes when I (Bob) have a week of night meet-ings, or I do the grocery shopping to help Deb during deadline time. Whatever it takes to let the other know that we want to make life a bit easier, we try to do it.

What are some "little things" you can do to secure your love?

- Write a love note. Place this on your mate's pillow to be discovered when he/she awakens in the morning.
- Gas up the car. Imagine how your mate will feel when she

doesn't have to worry about this task.

- Place some fresh flowers in a vase on your mate's bedside table. Even men like fresh flowers.
- Do your mate's chores when he is stressed or tired.
- Give your mate the preferred chair while watching TV. This tells her that she is important without actually saying it.
- Iron a shirt or dress. Balancing career and family can put all of us in overload. Taking a little pressure off during busy times will help your mate relax and feel loved.
- Affirm your mate's special accomplishments. A handwritten banner hung across your bed, a note on the refrigerator, or a colorful balloon tied to her chair are all ways to affirm.
- Pray for your mate. When words fail you, lift your mate up in prayer daily. Pray for his/her needs and shortcomings and thank God for this amazing miracle of life in your best friend.
- Write a lunchbox note. Everyone likes to see the words "I love you" when away from home.
- Take a lunch by the office and have lunch together.
- Meet for dinner on the way home from work on the spur of the moment.
- Send flowers for no reason.
- Send balloons for no reason.
- Plan a surprise evening or weekend away.
- Cuddle while watching TV. (It's important for children to see parents being affectionate too.)
- Give a back rub.
- Hug your mate frequently. Hugs are forgiving, especially when you both feel unlovable.
- Share favorite Scriptures. Sensing your mate's concerns, write down Scriptures on file cards that apply to his/her needs and place them where they will be seen. The words may give assurance at the right moment.
- Serve your mate breakfast in bed once in a while.
- Worship together regularly. Attending church with your

mate on a regular basis affirms that Jesus Christ is important in your life.

Long-term relationships need a boost now and then. Problems arise in marriages when "the little things" stop taking place. In talking with men and women who have been married more than ten years, we have found that the men tend to stop making romantic gestures after the courtship stage has passed, and women often stop showing appreciation for the little things their spouse does for them. When a man feels taken for granted he often reacts with withdrawal. Small gestures bring big rewards to your romance. Pause in your busy lives and take time to show your love for each other.

"But Jack's not very good at that," Patricia complained when we shared how small gestures throughout the day could make a big difference when it comes to making love. Most men are not very creative when it comes to surprising their wife, whether with love notes, poetry, or gifts. But that does not mean that they cannot be taught to take time throughout the day to think, *What is it that would make my wife smile today?*

Clinical psychologist Judith Sills claims that this pleasure-giving has a rebound effect. As you show a giving gesture toward your husband (or wife), you feel more loving toward him/her, and love is what you want to feel for the partner with whom you share your life. Your touch on his cheek, your note in his desk, the candy you place in the glove compartment are all gifts to yourself as well. Sure, they make him feel loved, and that is very nice. But they make you feel loving—which is even nicer.[11]

Week Four: Make Time for Romance

Focus: Sex in marriage is part of God's plan for men and women. But before you can experience sexual satisfaction in your relationship, you must relearn how to touch each other in a manner that communicates caring and affection, how to break barriers that have built up through the years, and how to make time to be alone.

Central Bible Truth: "That the husband and wife are one body is proved by the Scripture that says, 'A man must leave his father and mother when he marries, so that he can be perfectly joined to his wife, and the two shall be one' " (Ephesians 5:31).

Monday: *Role Mates or Soulmates?*

To reclaim intimacy in our relationships, we must be aware of the emotional differences between men and women. Men need intimacy along with a certain amount of independence and autonomy. When a man has separated enough, he will feel his need for love and intimacy again and will come springing back to his wife or partner. Women are motivated when they feel cherished and respected. When a woman is not cherished, she becomes compulsively responsible and exhausted from too much giving. By listening empathetically to your wife without trying to fix things or trying to change her, you will help to keep love alive. We cannot expect our partners to satisfy all our needs and desires. Some of this satisfaction must come from within. When we work on our inner person, we increase our self-esteem and self-worth. When men and women are open and honest about each other, when they can express their joys and sorrows to one another, their relationship can become more intimate physically and emotionally.

Reflection and response:

After reading Chapter 4, how would you describe your re-lationship—as Role Mates or Soulmates? Are both partners happy with this description? If so, why? If not, write down your feelings along with some suggestions both can work on to effect change.

His: _____

_____

Hers: _____

_____

Tuesday: *Lean on the little things.*

It is the little things in our own marriage that add up to an exciting relationship. In fact, we work daily at making life better for the other person—even when we don't feel like being loving or helpful or considerate.

Reflection and response:

In your marriage, what areas need to be strengthened so both partners fill supported and fulfilled? What little things can you do to help your partner have more free time? More energy? More time together? Write these here:

His: _____

_____

Hers: _____

_____

Wednesday: *Rediscover touch.*

Touch is vital to experiencing physical closeness. We are not speaking here of sexual touch, but rather stroking, back rubs, gentle touches on the arms, the lips, the face.

Reflection and response:

Lie down together sometime today when there are no distractions or children around to interrupt you. Spend time in nonsexual touch: a back rub, touching fingers, gentle strokes on the face. Let this physical closeness be a loving way to communicate your intimate feelings. Write how you feel after this touch experience.

His: _____

_____

Hers: _____

_____

Thursday: *Romance starts in the kitchen.*

Being romantic with your partner does not mean that you say just the right words or perform a specific action. Being romantic occurs when you and your partner see yourselves as appreciated and loved—outside of the bedroom. Sex is primarily a cerebral act, which is why we often say that "romance starts in the kitchen."

Because sex in marriage is a type of "adult play," it is important to build up to this moment by enjoying each other outside the bedroom. A good sexual relationship depends on the ability to relax and enjoy each other. We know that problems occur when one partner is carrying too much of a load, whether working long hours away from the home, or doing all of the household duties, including caring for the children. When this is true, it is difficult to have a satisfying sex life, because one of you is always exhausted.

Reflection and response:

Before you leave for work, start the morning off by working together at home, whether making beds, cooking dinner, or washing dishes side-by-side. While you are job sharing, enjoy each other's presence. Give signals that you are each important to the other by touching his arm, giving her a warm hug, and smiling intentionally at your partner. Do these body signals give a warm, caring message to your spouse? Do you receive these as such? Did they enable you to feel more sexual later in the day? Write your feelings here:

His: _____

_____

Hers: _____

_____

Friday: *Enjoy each other.*

For centuries people have known that humor and health are closely tied together. Even in biblical times, writers reported that "A cheerful heart does good like medicine" (Proverbs 17:22). A really good belly laugh helps your muscles to relax (except in your face and abdomen), and even more importantly, it seems to strengthen your immune system, and good health is important to all of us. Some studies have shown that people who laugh hard produce more immunoglobulin A, which fights against upper respiratory infections. Your heart rate increases, the oxygen to the brain is boosted, and your blood flow improves. When you relax afterward, your body calms down.

Reflection and response:

How often do you and your partner laugh with each other? Do you ever take time to watch a funny TV show or share comical stories with each other? Tonight, rent a video that is strictly humor and watch this alone—no kids allowed. Did laughter help to break down relationship barriers and enable you to feel physically close?

His: _____

_____

Hers: _____

_____

Saturday: *Ignite the flames of intimacy.*

It is also important to let the other know how very much you love him/her. Mother Teresa says, "If we want a love message to be heard, it has got to be sent out. To keep a lamp burning, we have to keep putting oil in it." The same is true in cultivating an intimate relationship.

In order to reclaim the romantic passion you once felt, you need to recapture the mind-set you had then—the anticipation of being with this new love, the warmth and excitement when you were together, and the sadness you experienced when you had to say goodbye.

Reflection and response:

Look through photo albums of when you first met, and talk about feelings you had toward each other then. How have they changed? As you spend time together tonight, try to recapture some of the excitement and newness you felt before your marriage. Write down any changes you wish to make in your sexual relationship here:

His: _____

_____

Hers: _____

_____

Sunday: *Explore the seven levels of love.*

Dr. Barbara de Angelis tells of seven levels of love that need to be included when making time for romance with your spouse.[12] All of these areas need nurturing in order to experience total sexual fulfillment in a marriage. Write how you and your partner are meeting each other's needs within each level of love:

1. Physical: sports, walks, dancing, touch, other.

_____

_____

2. Recreational: things done just for fun—films, games, sightseeing, music, social activities.

_____

_____

3. Sexual: talking about sex, being affectionate, and creating intimate times.

_____

_____

4. Educational: learning new things together—seminars, lectures, sharing a book, creating a recipe.

_____

_____

5. Intellectual: sharing your mind with your partner; discussion of politics, biblical studies, and other important matters.

_____

_____

6. Emotional: time just to nurture each other and to support the other in the changes he or she is going through.

_____

_____

7. Spiritual: sharing your experience of spiritual matters together; attending worship; praying together, sharing faith, going for a silent walk together.

_____

_____

Reflection and response:

Looking at the seven levels of love, what areas are you strong in? What areas do you and your partner need to work on?

His: _____

_____

Hers: _____

_____

5

WEEK FIVE
Stop the Fast Track to Marital Failure

We must make a confession upfront before we talk about how effective time management is for strengthening intimacy in your marriage. This book is written by two recovering workaholics. Now you may wonder, *If they were workaholics, what can they teach us?* We hope to teach you a great deal, for we have found that lack of time is not the stumbling block to achieving intimacy in marriage; rather, it is a lack of commitment to do what really matters, including spending time with God, our husband or wife, and our children.

Twelve years ago, we were so exhausted from overextending ourselves that we lacked the energy needed to emotionally charge our relationship. Marriage invaders were common for us and the list was long—stress, overwork, too much community involvement, active kids, and more. In our two-career family, we found it virtually impossible to juggle all of the pieces of our lives. But when life's interruptions occurred, such as a child with chronic health problems, a sudden move to another city, and the death of a close friend, we were unprepared to cope.

While we have cheated ourselves of precious time together in years past, we have learned how to overcome this and want to tell the good news, that you can learn to balance your work and your life while maintaining an intimate relationship with God, with each other, and with your family. We know personally that intimacy takes time, involvement, and often sacrifice.

A Hurried Society

You may be familiar with the time-honored story about the board meeting that Satan called in hell. He put this question to his senior advisors: "We need to develop a new strategy for causing havoc on earth. Do you have any new suggestions for reaching human beings for our side?"

One advisor suggested, "Tell them there is no heaven."

Another said, "Tell them there is no hell."

But the prize-winning suggestion was judged to be much more effective: "Tell them there is no hurry."

How many of us in our hurry-sick society wouldn't love to live somewhere where the rule was: "No hurry allowed"? One hurried friend we know can read the newspaper, watch the news, listen to a ball game on the radio, eat dinner, and carry on a conversation with his spouse. Now tell us that intimacy isn't also hurried in his relationship!

While it seems that the busier our lives become, the more difficult it is to complete everything, the real problem lies in how well we manage our time. Haven't you known people who seem to accomplish an incredible amount of work each day, yet still seem to "have it all together"? We have. Sherri not only is the mother of three active children, but she is also a respected high school principal in our community. Sherri definitely is busy, but she also has learned how to set priorities and choose which tasks are important and must be addressed immediately and which tasks can wait for later attention.

We know that if you are a busy mother or father, time seems to be of the essence. A study by Bryn Mawr College fifty years ago stated that women devoted more than eighty hours a week to cleaning the house, cooking meals, and taking care of the children. With all of our modern technology, have things improved? You know the answer to that.

Another study taken twenty-five years ago reported that full-time homemakers spent more hours doing laundry in the 1970s than they did in the 1920s, despite all the new washing machines, dryers, detergents, stain removers, and bleaches. The main change was that the family had acquired more clothing and now had even higher expectations about cleanliness and grooming.

In the 1990s, few women can even afford to dream of devoting full-time attention to their families. Thus, the extraordinary demands of running a home are added to running an office or a classroom or a business. Where does the time go?

This time crunch has even hit the medical field. A University of Michigan study found that one third of all physicians in the United States are so busy working that they are two years behind the breakthroughs in their own field. That is a scary truth. As the Queen of Hearts said in *Alice in Wonderland*, "It takes all the running you can do to keep in the same place. If you want to get somewhere else, you must run at least twice as fast as that!"

We disagree with the Queen of Hearts! We feel that men and women today can get the very things done that are important to them and still have intimate time together. Yet while the goal of most successful people is to get "more done with less," don't most of us feel that we run around twice as fast as others, getting less done in more time? It doesn't have to be this way.

Exploration:

Do you have a problem with time management? Review the following time crunches with your partner and check off those that apply to you:

His   **Hers**

_____ _____ My time is not my own.

_____ _____ I am under chronic overload and always have more to do than I have time available.

_____ _____ I have difficulty separating work and home.

_____ _____ I lose concentration when I'm with my spouse because I'm always thinking about other things I have to do.

_____ _____ I have difficulty delegating to my spouse or children, so I do it all myself.

_____ _____ I do not know how to say "no" to church or community activities that put me in overload. There is no time in my day for exercise.

_____ _____ I never seem to finish at the office, so I bring my work home.

_____ _____ I stay awake at night anticipating the next day's problems and am too tense to be physically intimate.

How did you score? If you checked more than three time crunches, you need to keep reading and prepare to do some homework. As you and your partner begin to rethink living in the fast lane, it is important to learn to balance your life—that is, weighing your obligations with the amount of time in each day and choosing to do the very things that really matter. Remember the old saying that no one on his deathbed ever wished he had spent more time at the office.

Healing the Workaholic

While most of us know what compulsive and addictive behavior is, has it ever occurred to you that this behavior could be operative in your family? We're talking about the husband or wife who compulsively works long hours, ignoring those who love them most. Most of these people would deny that their behavior is compulsive or addictive and would claim that if they were to win the lottery tomorrow, they would readily demonstrate a different lifestyle. Don't believe it!

It is important to note that workaholics are both men and women, employed and unemployed, young and old. Yes, workaholics can be found in all walks of life. The homemaker who feels compelled to keep a spotless house, cook gourmet meals, bake her own bread, and iron the sheets and underwear may be a workaholic when her actions are addictive/compulsive and interfere with the rest of her life and relationships. People tend to spend their time where they receive the most satisfaction and approval. This means that for some, shiny sinks bring more reinforcement than a hurried spouse.

The workaholic typically comes from a family where he enjoyed the role of being the "good" kid and where being successful was valued and promoted. The fear of not being good enough or disappointing someone literally drives him to keep working in order to hide his deep feelings of inadequacy and "messing up."

Dealing With Relationships

Predictably the workaholic usually develops problems in intimate relationships (spouse, children, close friends) because functionally priorities are out of balance. Often the workaholic's spouse practices the same co-dependent behavior as the alcoholic's spouse (making constant excuses to others to explain such things as canceled dinner parties, or rationalizing to oneself over a lack of commitment to the relationship—"He works so hard and is just too tired to have sex.").

Frequent arguing, communication difficulties, or feelings of loneliness and isolation become identifiable problems in relationships. Essential to bringing about change is the understanding that working hard provides an emotional payoff to the workaholic and that the family system often supports the dysfunction.[1]

Fran Tarkenton has said that Americans have carried the work ethic too far. "The real reason behind this is that people would probably rather be at their offices than at home. Office problems are easier to deal with—they are not emotional. We have reinforced work time more than work performance. I think just the opposite of that theory is true. The quality of time we spend away from work is as important as the quality of time we spend on work. I need—as we all do—time away from the office environment to go fishing or play golf or climb mountains because that is when I come up with my greatest thoughts. I get the cobwebs out. I refurbish myself and come back twice as productive."[2]

Urgency for What Really Matters

While we shouldn't follow the path of a workaholic in order to get things done in life, there is built into life an important urgency when it comes to the things that really matter— such as your eternal relationship with Christ Jesus. Can you recall one Scripture in the New Testament where Jesus told people to "go home, think it over, and get back to me tomorrow"? It simply is not that way. We read in Matthew 4 that Jesus went to Simon, Andrew, James, and John at their fishing boats beside the Sea of Galilee and said to them, "Follow me."

Immediately they left their nets and followed him. Matthew tells us that James and John left their father and followed him. Jesus' invitation is always an invitation to do it now.

Life seems to pass by so quickly, and so much of it is wasted because we do not have a center for our lives, a divine direction. Paul says, "I myself no longer live, but Christ lives in me" (Galatians 2:20). This means that if we will let him, Christ will direct our lives and make us effective in everything we do. When we are in Christ, we are fulfilling our divine direction; Christ Jesus gives us a center.

Steps to Stopping the Fast Track to Marital Failure

We have found that because our marriage is now centered in Christ Jesus, we are so much more effective than we used to be in the use of our time. We want to honor him in all we do, and being good stewards of our time is one way we do this. But for too many people, time together—that precious binding glue of marriages—is at an all-time low. Everything from careers to commuting time to the extraordinary explosion of leisure-time options (video, computers, self-improvement, adult education, television) means that the time left over for sustaining the relationship is shrinking, not expanding. But there is help for the spouse who needs to cut back at work in order to give more to the marriage, or the spouse who needs to let go of the house or outside commitments to spend more intimate time with her mate.

Let the following steps help you prioritize what is most important in your life as you become centered in Christ Jesus and balance your commitments outside the family with those that are most meaningful: God, your marriage, and your children.

Step 1: *Set limits in your lives.*

To live responsibly in life, we must know our boundaries. This means we must understand our commitments and weigh these with our ability to perform.

Start by making priorities. Somewhere in life we have to set priorities; that is, we must decide what really matters and make certain that the really important things are done. Time with our husbands and wives, service to our community, attention to our work, relaxation, self-improvement—we could develop a list of important issues that would go on and on, but somewhere we all must draw the line.

In our marriage, our first priority is obedience to God. We feel that if we are too busy to hear God's voice, then we are just too busy. We must not forget that there will become a time when our relationship with Him will be the only priority that will matter.

Do a reality check. The first reality is that there are only twenty-four hours in each day—no more, no less. Of those twenty-four hours, depending on how much you sleep, you have available to you from sixteen to eighteen hours of actual time awake. The other reality is that you are human and have limitations. Some of us are able to handle a greater workload than others and still make free time to spend with those we love. But we have found that most people work harder than necessary to enjoy what life has to give.

Write down all your commitments. Everyone claims to be overcommitted, but few take the time to do something about it. Most people wait until a crisis hits them in the face before they get control of their responsibilities. With your spouse, make lists of all the commitments you both have, including God and each other as the top priorities. On this list also write down the very commitments that put you in overload, such as serving on that steering committee for school, or being the telephone person for all three children's classes.

As we began this process of prioritizing our time, we realized that what stresses one person does not bother the other. For example, Deb (the early bird) detests night meetings. Before she got a handle on time management, she had generously volunteered for several church and school committees that met until 9:00 or 10:00 at night. While she enjoyed the involvement and the goals of the committees, staying up late took its toll on her commitment to the family. Invariably, she would wake up the next day feeling grumpy and out-of-sorts. I (Bob, the nocturnal animal) am just coming alive at night, so making evening commitments works well with my body rhythms. We learned to adjust commitments to suit our personal needs and our marital needs.

Prioritize your commitments. After you have made your list of commitments, divide this list into two sections: YES (these are the commitments you must keep) and MAYBE (these are the commitments that are not as important or that you can change).

For most of us, staying employed is a major commitment we all must keep in order to put food on the table, but working late into the evening hours or working seven days a week is a commitment we can and must change.

Ben's Sample Priority List

YES (Must Do)	MAYBE (Flexible)
obedience to God	bowling night with guys
being with Mary Jane	Saturday football games (TV)
being with kids	surfing the Internet
career goals	painting garage
disciple Bible class	softball game at church league
daily walk with Mary Jane	basketball on Sunday night
family dinners	extra project at work

Make necessary changes. What changes do you need to make in your list of priorities? Work on what you can change (MAYBE list), and accept what you cannot (YES list). Just be sure to moderate the time spent on all commitments so that your top priorities, including God, spouse, and children, are included. On Ben's list, he found that he could moderate watching sports on TV at night and weekends and have more time to spend with Mary Jane and their children. Instead of painting the garage and reorganizing his workroom, he put off that project for three months to coach TJ's T-ball team. He learned to prioritize what was most important in life and follow through with that commitment.

Set reasonable—not perfect—expectations. Are you always struggling to achieve the best in whatever you do? While our calling to Christian discipleship demands that we do our best, a constant push for perfection can cause undue stress, which results in hazards to our mental and physical well-being.

We have experienced that one of the biggest stumbling blocks of trying to be perfect is that you develop unrealistic expectations of yourself. These expectations can become self-defeating when events and persons outside of your control thwart your perfection. Having to be perfect may become a form of trying to earn your way into God's favor. In doing so you may block the grace of God in your life. Perfectionism can be a burden when you don't allow yourself the risky necessity of making mistakes.

The Bible recognizes perfectionism as an issue for Christians. Jesus commanded us to be perfect, and Paul recognized our imperfection: "Now we know so little, even with our special gifts, and the preaching of those most gifted is still so poor. But when we have been made perfect and complete, then the need for these inadequate special gifts will come to an end, and they will disappear" (1 Corinthians 13:9–10). Again in Philippians 3:7-14, Paul said that he was not already perfect, but that he was pressing on to become something more. Christians are to rate their ability with sober judgment, each according to the degree of faith apportioned by God to them (Romans 12:3–8).

Realize that as a human being you are imperfect, and yet as a person of faith you are pressing on to become something more than you are now. Knowing this tension, you can begin to make some changes in your expectations of yourself. These changes can help you relax so that you can enjoy God's grace at work in you to bring you to wholeness and well-being.

Develop a marital mission statement. A marital mission statement is important to increase the intimacy in your relationship as you get a handle on where you spend your time. This represents the very heart of both partners as you write down what is most important to you—the direction your lives are heading. Your mission statement may be something like ours, which reads, "Our mission as Bob and Deb is to grow daily in love for God, for each other, for our children, and for those around us; to balance this intimate love with care of self, doing the very things that complete our lives and our dreams—separately and together; and to give back to God's world without taking away from our partner."

Our mission statement helps give purpose to our relationship, especially when one partner becomes overly committed with outside obligations and needs to refocus.

Rethink your life together. When Bob felt God's call to the ministry, it was during our engagement period. While I (Deb) was supportive of this life commitment, I also had some reserves. "Just promise me," I said, "that you won't do mission work while we are raising children." And Bob made that vow. While mission work is eternally rewarding to those in service to God, we negotiated this marital stumbling block in order to become as one in our thinking and in our lives.

We have found that all the individual life dreams mean nothing unless you and your partner are making life decisions together; only then can dreams become reality.

Review your priority list weekly. Learning to get a handle on time management does not happen with just one intimate meeting. This is something you will need to go over week after week. Unfortunately, many couples tell of problems doing this because while they can change their own behavior, they cannot change that of their spouse. With that in mind, it is important to be assertive and communicate with your spouse if you find that priorities are out of control. This means telling him or her exactly how you feel about overcommitment in an honest and respectful manner.

Make a daily to-do list. Get in the habit of writing down your daily obligations as soon as you get up each day. I (Deb) like to write my list in the evening, as I reflect on what didn't get accomplished that day and move this to the next day's to-do list. Bob writes his daily list on 3×5 file cards and carries these around with him, checking off commitments after he has completed them.

Set aside time for each other. We've become a sad society when we actually have to schedule time to be with our mates, but it is important. Put your mate's name at the top of your to-do list and write down ways you want to be with him/her that day.

Step 2: *Stop procrastinating.*

Procrastination is probably the single biggest time-management problem for most of us, but it can be stopped . . . if you act now. Many procrastinators are perfectionists just waiting for the "perfect" time to accomplish the task, yet others claim they perform better "under the gun." But procrastination only adds to the stress you face each day. You can stop this time-stealer if you learn to set your priorities, schedule tasks for peak efficiency, and establish attainable goals that will lessen your frustration and failure.

Most procrastinators need to do self-reflection; that is, they should be realistic about what needs to be done and how long it will take. For example, if you or your spouse procrastinates about cleaning the whole house on Saturdays, break it up into small pieces. Doing fifteen minutes here or fifteen minutes there will get the job done adequately, and you won't have to live with the panic and stress of "Oh, dear, I've only got two hours to do the whole thing!"

Deb used to procrastinate with her writing, until our children were born. Try to write books with three active preschoolers and a dog running circles around you—it's not easy. She learned that in order to alleviate the stress of publisher's deadlines, she formed her personal deadlines. If a manuscript was due on June 14, she would boost that deadline up three or four weeks and make it due on May 21. This gave her some built-in leeway, just in case a child got sick or other emergencies occurred. This plan worked to end her procrastination and she has never missed a deadline since.

Learn to do what is most important (checking back to your YES list), then procrastinate on your MAYBE list—doing the less important tasks as you find time. This will allow you to feel less stress as you know that your major priorities are completed.

Step 3: *Get proper sleep.*

"I've never heard that sleep can enhance intimacy in marriage!" Josh said recently. This forty-two-year-old husband and father of four was a prime example of how restful sleep *could* improve his intimate relationship with Kate, his wife. Not only did he burn the candles at both ends, trying to maintain a marketing consulting firm while moonlighting at night teaching courses at the junior college, Josh spent weekends coaching soccer teams, teaching Sunday school, and going over his financial records for work. And what was Kate's greatest complaint about their twenty-year marriage? "Josh is always tired."

If you are having trouble sleeping at night, you have company: most adults over age forty express the same problem—a problem that worsens with age. One study found that Americans cut their sleep time by 20 percent in the last century. This reduction of sleep time is a problem for the majority of adults who need seven hours of sleep each night. One study found that those adults who slept only six hours each night experienced more frequent health problems, and over a period of nine years, these shorter sleepers had a 70 percent higher mortality rate.

But it's not always easy to get a good night's sleep, especially as our bodies age and our responsibilities grow. As our normal quality of sleep changes with aging, we are more prone to develop disorders that can disrupt or even ruin peaceful slumber. In fact, perhaps you know from personal experience the out-of-sorts and dragging feeling you experience when you lose sleep.

Anything that influences our body will also affect our mind. Disrupted sleep not only affects how you feel physically, but it can create a weakened emotional state. Let's face it. Who can be intimate with someone else when you feel out-of-sorts and grouchy from interrupted sleep? But this becomes an even greater problem when you are faced with life's interruptions. The death of a loved one, financial problems, a troubled child—all of these problems happen whether we are rested or not.

If you have difficulty sleeping because of poor time management, first get your priorities in order, then try the following helpful suggestions:

- Get adequate sleep each night. Some people lose sleep all week, then try to make up for it on the weekend. This only disrupts your body's circadian rhythm. The term "circadian" is derived from *circa*, meaning approximately, and *die*, meaning day. These body rhythms are separate, individually synchronized internal rhythms that affect our daily sleep cycles, performance and alertness, moods, and even gastro-intestinal function.
- Wake up at the same time every day, weekday or weekend. This strengthens your circadian cycle—your daily rhythmicity—and will help to establish regular sleep patterns.
- Use earplugs if you are bothered by noises while sleeping. Some people find that "white noise"—a machine that produces a humming sound or a radio set to a station that has gone off the air—helps.
- Hunger may disrupt your sleep. Eat a snack high in car-

bohydrates to lull you to dreamland. Sometimes crackers, sherbet, or a bagel may help to relax you.

- Caffeine disturbs sound sleep. Avoid caffeine after noon each day, or if you are sensitive to caffeine, make plans to eliminate this from your diet.
- Continue your regular exercise program. But avoid doing this late in the day as it might stimulate you and make falling asleep difficult.
- Avoid napping during the day. If you need to rest, sit up in a chair and listen to music or read a book. Naps can disturb sleep at nighttime.

Week Five: Stop the Fast Track to Marital Failure

Focus: At a marriage seminar we attended many years ago, a story was told of J. Paul Getty. Getty was perhaps the richest man in the world, and there was no question about the fact that his "winning attitude" had taken him all the way to the top. Along the way, Getty had been married five times, all five marriages ending in divorce. He once told an interviewer: "I would give up all my wealth for one successful marriage. I hate not being able to make a success of marriage." Getty blamed himself for the divorces, saying, "No wife enjoys feeling that she is playing a minor supporting role to a corporate balance sheet."

Intimacy in marriage takes time. Intimacy means that we choose to invest ourselves in what we care about. Use these actions this week to put your energies back into your marriage instead of dividing your time with so many intrusions. Learn to cut back on unnecessary activities and commitments and give more time to things that matter—your intimate relationship.

Central Bible Truth: "For where your treasure is, there will your heart be also" (Matthew 6:21, RSV).

Monday: *Where do you spend your time?*

Use the following form to write down what you do in a typical day. Be sure to include eating, sleeping, watching TV, working, and daydreaming. Look this over at the end of the day and reflect on any "time-zappers." Continue to record your daily time expenditures throughout this week, using your journal.

Reflection and response:

No one puts pressure on you—except you. Looking at your schedule, do you find time gaps where you could have made better use of your time? List some of the intrusions that occupied your time:

His: _____

_____

Hers: _____

_____

Daily Worksheet

His		Hers
_____	6–7 A.M.	_____
_____	7–8 A.M.	_____
_____	8–9 A.M.	_____
_____	9–10 A.M.	_____
_____	10–11 A.M.	_____
_____	11–12 P.M.	_____
_____	12–1 P.M.	_____
_____	1–2 P.M.	_____
_____	2–3 P.M.	_____
_____	3–4 P.M.	_____

_____	4–5 P.M.	_____
_____	5–6 P.M.	_____
_____	6–7 P.M.	_____
_____	7–8 P.M.	_____
_____	8–9 P.M.	_____
_____	9–10 P.M.	_____
_____	10–11 P.M.	_____
_____	11–12 A.M.	_____
_____	12–1 A.M.	_____
_____	1–2 A.M.	_____
_____	2–3 A.M.	_____
_____	3–4 A.M.	_____
_____	4–5 A.M.	_____
_____	5–6 A.M.	_____

Tuesday: *Are you a workaholic?*

Look at the following list and check off those that pertain to you. Are you or your partner a workaholic?

- You love those 12–15 hours a day at the office.
- You always have a briefcase full of papers to review.
- You need to stay up after everyone has gone to bed to finish one more project.
- You haven't had a vacation in years, and the last time you went you couldn't wait to get home and get back to work.
- You used to enjoy the beach with your family, boating, dancing, hiking, or other, but haven't had the time lately.
- You find Sundays difficult to endure.
- You can't relax.
- At home, your thoughts are on what needs to be done at the office.
- You feel pressured or angry about money.
- Your spouse and kids don't really know you anymore, and for that matter, you don't know them very well either.

- You haven't been truly intimate with your spouse in months.
- Your kids are having problems in school.
- You are not feeling appreciated or understood.
- You may be eating and/or drinking too much.
- You may be thinking about or wishing for an affair.
- You promise to slow down but never do.[3]

Reflection and response:

After reviewing the list, talk about the problems of over-commitment in your marriage. What solutions can you think of that would help the workaholic cut back and give more time to things that matter? Write these down:

His: _____

_____

Hers: _____

_____

Wednesday: *Stop procrastinating.*

Do you procrastinate? Procrastination only adds to your daily stress as you wait until the last minute to get tasks completed. But procrastination can be halted using the time-management steps described in this chapter.

Reflection and response:

Name three things you have avoided doing this week, and write down the reasons why you procrastinated on these. Some ideas could be reading the Bible, being with your spouse alone, or doing a household chore that you dread. How can you change this behavior? What is holding you back from doing this?

His: _____

_____

Hers: _____

_____

Thursday: *Get adequate sleep.*

Don't most of the people you know have the same thing in common—that is, they are always tired? We are a tired generation. But in the midst of wanting to get the most out of every day of our lives, we forget that we are human and have very human needs; specifically, we need restful sleep in order to feel recharged and healthy the next day.

Reflection and response:

How many hours have you slept this week? Write down how many hours you slept on the following nights: Monday, Tuesday, Wednesday. What is holding you back from getting adequate sleep? Do you feel rested in the morning and throughout the day? Following the steps in this chapter, plan on an early night tonight with your spouse to ensure sound sleep. Write down how you feel when you are not rested:

His: _____

_____

Hers: _____

_____

Friday: *Enjoy a daydream.*

If only I had time, I would . . . How many times have you said this to someone? To yourself? If only I had the time, I would learn to play the piano. If only I had the time, I would learn to speak another language. The list goes on. Does life have a hold on you, or are you in charge of how you spend your time?

Reflection and response:

If this is a clear day, go out into your backyard (or a park) with your spouse, spread out a blanket, and lie down together to watch the clouds. Talk aloud about things you would do together . . . if only you had the time. Let your imagination take over and daydream aloud. Write down some of these things you wish to do.

His: _____

_____

Hers: _____

_____

Saturday: *Break bad habits.*

What are some bad habits that interfere with effective time management? Brian told of being addicted to his son's computer games and instead of setting aside time to talk with his wife, he was glued to the computer. No one controls habits but ourselves.

Reflection and response:

List three bad habits that rob you of time alone with your spouse. What habits take your time? Some ideas include TV sports, sitcoms, and the telephone.

His: _____

_____

Hers: _____

_____

Sunday: *Renew your commitment to each other.*

As we shared, urgency is important where salvation is concerned. Especially when our lives are full of turmoil and no end is in sight, turning to Christ Jesus and asking for strength, hope, and encouragement can give you inner peace.

Reflection and response:

Only God can help you get your priorities straight. Freedom from the stress and anxieties of a hurried life can only happen when we move beyond "self" and turn humbly to the Lord for guidance. Only he can free us from the bondage of an overcommitted and meaningless life.

Using the information on page 135, design your own marital mission statement. Pray together that God will give you the strength to implement this. Write your mission statement here:

Marital Mission Statement

_____

_____

_____

_____

6

WEEK SIX

De-Stress Your Life

Your week has come to an end. Not only did your child come down with chicken pox, but the washer broke, the neighbor's dog dug up your new azaleas, and your boss called to say you need to catch up on some work—all day Saturday.

How do you handle life's stressors? Do you reach out and socialize with others? Or, do you lock your door and hide?

If you're like us, you probably enjoy spending time with family in your home, your cocoon, or shelter from the harried world. After a stressful week of dealing with kids, commitments, and career, we both long for those quiet nights with our family when we finally deadbolt the doors and protect ourselves from the intrusions of life. Our motto oftentimes is "call us homebodies . . . but please don't call us!"

We're definitely not alone. Cocooning is epidemic among millions of folks today. It's no news that for most people, life is confused, disorganized, frustrating, and, to be honest, quite difficult. But have we created such a stressed-out society that the only way we can cope is to hide?

According to Florida-based pastoral counselor Rev. Bill Scott, cocooning gives isolation or protection from life's stressors. "There are two basic types of people in the world: introverts and extroverts," Scott contends. "One of the differences between the introverts and extroverts is what they do to regroup and relax or how they recharge their batteries after doing battle in today's world."

Scott finds that extroverts get their batteries recharged by going to a party or a ball game, while introverts recharge their batteries by giving space to themselves or simply by being alone. "For introverts, cocooning is a beneficial experience because it is their way of relaxing and regrouping. Extroverts don't cocoon because a desire to be alone or withdraw is not in their nature."[1]

We're a Burned-Out Generation

Perhaps cocooning can be blamed on our introvert or extrovert nature. Or, perhaps it is because most of us are all on the brink of burnout; therefore we cocoon to seek refuge from our stressed lives. A recent poll by the Gallup Organization revealed that for more than half of those aged 35 to 54—stress is a frequent part of their daily lives, listing job and financial problems as the leading stressors.[2] For those who work outside of the home, even when they leave the office for the day, downtime is often spent negotiating deals with clients on cellular phones or answering faxes and e-mail at home. Whether you deal with downsizing, mergers, and layoffs, or kids, car-pools, and housework, it is no news that many of us work twenty-four hours a day, seven days a week—even when we are not officially "at work."

Yes, stress is an issue for most of us today. But how have we learned to turn off life's intrusions? It's simple. For many of us, we turn off the phone and lock the door; we cocoon during our downtime.

Our Social Network Is Gone

Some sociologists claim that cocooning is a widespread symptom of a transient society where people have lost their social network. In years past, people lived close to family members and relied on parents and siblings for affirmation and emotional strength, even after marriage. When suffering occurred, people could turn to relatives for comfort and support. But with our highly mobile society, most adults today live hundreds of miles away from parents and siblings. We are not used to having our doorbell ring at all hours of the day or having extended family members living next door or even in our homes.

But this social support that our ancestors experienced is important. Close relationships with family and friends allow us to nourish our hungry souls. When we are tied emotionally to those we love, we can let out our feelings of fear, insecurity, and guilt and receive comfort from people who accept us—just as we are—with no strings attached. But if we have no place that feels safe enough to let down our emotional defenses, then we tend to keep our guard up all the time—a dissatisfied and troubled guard that numbly masks the very afflictions we are facing.

While cocooning may help us feel less stressful as we withdraw after a busy work week, it certainly does not offer protection against stress. Research on stress-resistant personality traits has identified certain keys to staying healthy. These include

- involvement in work or other tasks that have great meaning;
- the ability to relate well to others;
- and the ability to interact in a strong social network.

More and more studies in the field of phychoneuroimmunology (PNI or mind/body interplay) are finding that the people most vulnerable to illness are those who are socially isolated.

"Wait a minute!" you might say. "I thought I was de-stressing by shutting out society and all its problems."

In study after study, the findings were the same; that is, people with many social contacts—a spouse, a close-knit family, a network of friends, church, or other group affiliations—lived longer and had better health. In fact, those who had few ties with other people died at rates two to five times higher than those with good social ties.[3]

According to one researcher, "Despite the potential for stress in close, personal relationships, it's becoming increasingly clear that healthy, long lives depend on strengthening our bonds with others. A full and rewarding social life can nourish the mind, the emotions, and the spirit, and good physical health depends as much on these aspects of ourselves as it does on a strong and well-functioning body."[4]

If used appropriately, taking time out is important in our hurried, fast-paced lives as we rekindle love, positive thinking, and physical energy. Jesus told the disciples, "Come to me and I will give you rest" (Matthew 11:28). This is an important tool we can use today, as rest is a safety valve from pressure.

Jesus set a good example for us when he retreated to be alone with God. When he prayed and meditated on the hillside, Jesus put aside daily concerns and asked God for new power for living. This time-out renewed his spirit and enabled him to live out his ministry. However, don't forget that after Jesus was rested, he went out again among the masses, healing, preaching, and teaching the Word of God.

The problem arises when we spend *too much* time alone. This can be a symptom of a greater problem—that of social isolation. On the one hand, you may be purposely avoiding some people or the stressors you have to face each day. In that case, you find your home a secure haven where you are not on display and where there are loved ones around to meet your needs. On the other hand, loss of desire to be with friends or to engage in any social activity may be symptoms of mild depression. In that case, professional help should be sought.

Steps to De-Stressing Your Life

Something to note about the effect of stress is the intimate connection between body and soul, the physical and the emotional. Stress is brought about by conflict between our inner and outer life, by the fatigue of our body that can no longer respond to the longings of our heart.[5]

Let's look at some practical ways to reduce stress levels that may be hindering intimate relationships in your life.

Step 1: *Identify your stress level.*

Stress is the word used to describe the many demands and pressures that we all experience to one degree or another each day. These demands require us to change or adapt in some fashion and may be physical or emotional in nature. For example, being stuck in slow-moving traffic requires that we change our expectations about arriving at our destination on time. Similarly, going through a critical job interview requires that we maintain a relaxed, yet self-assured and confident approach to do our best and make a good impression.

What is your personal reaction to stress? The problem in actuality is not the stressor itself, but our personal reaction to it. The initial impact of anxiety or stress on a relationship is always one of increased reactivity. When we are in reactive gear, we are driven by our feelings, without the ability to think about how we want to express them.[6]

It has been said that the stressor itself represents 10 percent of the problem of stress; the other 90 percent of the problem is our *reaction* to the stressor. When we are exposed to a stressful situation perceived as threatening, our bodies prepare for confrontation or escape. This physical response, known as the "fight-or-flight" response, is controlled by our hormones and nervous system. A rush of adrenaline prepares us to either fight the perceived threat or run from it. Our prehistoric ancestors felt this fight-or-flight response when faced with wild animals and other dangers of the ancient world. Today we may not be facing as many wild animals, but we encounter many modern stressors that will trigger this response.

In a life-threatening encounter—say with an armed attacker—it is appropriate to respond openly in any way we feel we can best protect ourselves. But when the stressor is our boss telling us to work overtime for a second weekend in a row after we have made important family plans, we have learned to control our emotional response in a "civilized" manner. While keeping our emotions under control in the boss's office is appropriate, we need to learn how to negotiate a workable solution in such situations, or we may carry around a good deal of anger toward our boss. If this is how we habitually deal with stress, then in time we are likely to develop physical symptoms that result from our fight-or-flight response turning inward.

Recognize warning signs. Stress symptoms vary greatly from one person to the next. Checkmark the following stress-warning signals to see if you are experiencing overload, then find out what is creating the stress in your life and deal with this in a positive way.[7]

Stress Warning Signals

Physical Symptoms

☐	headaches	☐	back pain
☐	indigestion	☐	tight neck, shoulders
☐	stomachaches	☐	racing heart
☐	sweaty palms	☐	restlessness
☐	sleep difficulties	☐	tiredness
☐	dizziness	☐	ringing in ears

Behavioral Symptoms

- [ ] excess smoking
- [ ] bossiness
- [ ] compulsive gum chewing
- [ ] critical attitude toward others
- [ ] grinding of teeth at night
- [ ] overuse of alcohol
- [ ] compulsive eating
- [ ] inability to get things done

Emotional Symptoms

- [ ] crying
- [ ] nervousness, anxiety
- [ ] boredom, no meaning to things
- [ ] edginess, ready to explode
- [ ] feeling powerless to change things
- [ ] feeling of pressure
- [ ] anger
- [ ] loneliness
- [ ] unhappiness for no reason
- [ ] easily upset

Cognitive Symptoms

- [ ] trouble thinking clearly
- [ ] forgetfulness
- [ ] lack of creativity
- [ ] memory loss
- [ ] inability to make decisions
- [ ] thoughts of running away
- [ ] constant worry
- [ ] loss of sense of humor

If you are experiencing a few of these characteristics, chances are good that your level of stress is excessive. If left untreated, stress can lead to permanent feelings of helplessness and ineffectiveness.

Identify and remove the stress. The main strategy in dealing with stress is to identify and remove or reduce the source. If your stress is from overwork, learn to delegate at your office or at home. Your stress may be from overextending yourself with outside commitments. Reread how to modify your priorities and put this plan into action.

There are many ways to overcome the effects of too much stress. It is helpful as you begin a program to regain time in your life and reduce stress to simply list what your goal is, and then write down the possible actions you can take to achieve your goal.

Use the following as an example:

Goal:

1. To avoid putting undue pressure on myself to take care of the world.

2. To spend more time with my husband (or wife) instead of cleaning or working.

3. To talk about my anger instead of keeping it to myself.

Possible actions:

1. Keep my priority planning list by the telephone so I know my commitments before someone calls asking for my time.

2. Make a list each morning of what must be done and what can wait; follow this list throughout the day and check off what is important so I have "together" time at night.

3. Set aside time this week to ventilate without attacking my husband (or wife).

After reading this chapter and learning the tools to decrease stress and anxiety, use the form on pages 161–163 to write down your stress-reduction goals and possible actions you can take to achieve these goals. Check this list each week.

Have you stayed with your plan? Is it working? If you have not followed the actions you wrote down, rethink your plan and start over.

Step 2: *Take action to control cocooning.*

If cocooning has become a barrier between you and the outside world, there are workable steps you can take to break out of this. First, recognize when you've set up hurdles in your relationships. If you have worked hard all week and make a decision to be alone with your family on Friday night, that is healthy. But when you stay home day and night, week after week, and pull out of social activities, you need to evaluate your behavior. Are you hiding from relationships? Are you overextended and have no energy to enjoy friends and family? Are you suffering from depression?

The second step is getting your priorities in order so you have time and energy for socializing. Freedom from the stress and anxieties of a hurried life can only happen when we move beyond "self" and turn humbly to the Lord for guidance. Only he can free us from the bondage of an overcommitted and meaningless life.

Lastly, as you cut back your commitments, start to focus on moving beyond yourself into the lives of others. Starting with one day a week, make plans to be with other people. This could involve inviting friends over for a cookout on Saturday afternoon, or going out to lunch after church on Sunday. Most of us get into the pattern of "doing nothing" and forget how invigorating it feels to be around other people.

Be selective. Victor Frankl was a successful Viennese psychiatrist before being imprisoned at a Nazi concentration camp. He subsequently became a living answer to the question of how it was that some prisoners survived disease and malnutrition and others succumbed. He said, "Unless a man wishes to drown, he has to become selective. That is to say, he has to become able to select when to turn on the TV set, when to turn it off, what books and journals to read, and what to throw away in the wastebasket. Selectiveness means that we have to be responsible for what is important and what is not, what is essential and what is not, what is valuable and what is not, what is meaningful and what is not. We have to be capable or become capable of such decision making."

Being selective involves deciding when cocooning is appropriate and when it becomes obsessive; only you can make that decision. The Reverend Jim Marth agrees that cocooning is a sign of the times, especially within the local church. But as a pastor, Rev. Marth told us that the biggest detriment for

Christians who cocoon is that oftentimes they cut themselves off from other Christians.

"That is when cocooning becomes a serious spiritual issue," Marth contends. "When we isolate ourselves from other Christians, it means that we are accepting less than what God has planned for us and less than what God will offer. In this regard, cocooning can create a barrier around us and our homes that blocks others from entering our lives."[8]

There is no denying that we are a hurried generation. In this regard, sometimes cocooning or taking time out for rekindling a harried spirit can be a gentle reprieve. But when taking time out or avoiding social contact creates a barrier around us, we need to learn practical tools to break out of the cocoon.

Step 3: *Work together to solve money troubles.*

Money troubles rank second as the most common reason why married couples seek divorce, according to Gallup. What tears couples apart is not necessarily the amount of money they have at their disposal, but differing attitudes about the money they do have and opinions on how it should be used.

In the 1930s, less than 20 percent of women in the United States worked outside the home. Today over 58 percent of mothers with children under the age of six leave to go to work each day. With the many two-career marriages today, use of money is certainly an issue that needs to be discussed, settled, and agreed upon in families in order for harmony to be experienced.

More month than money? "No matter how much we make, we can't live on it," a mother of three told us. We agree that nothing is more exasperating than paying bills and realizing that you have more month than money! But, as Christians, we are called to live within our means as we practice responsible stewardship.

Christian stewardship is a way of life, and Jesus is the perfect example for us to follow. Jesus used every moment of his life to glorify God; we must do the same. We are but temporary trustees. Don't we all enjoy the bounty of goods that God has provided? But did you know that everything—all that we have and are—belongs to God . . . including our earnings? You see, God has made us the temporary trustees for his world; in fact, he gives us the power to receive these earnings. (Read Deuteronomy 8:17–18).

Consider tithing as a means of Christian stewardship. Personally, we believe that the biblical guideline for giving to Christ's Church is the tithe—10 percent of your income. Others insist that tithing is not the Church's method for raising money, but tithing is God's way of raising Christians! People who tithe agree and tell how this discipline has greatly deepened their faith and personal Christian commitment.

The Bible teaches us to set aside "our first fruits"—not what is leftover—to express love and gratitude for God's blessings. When you pay your tithe first—before anyone else is paid—and learn to live on the 90 percent that is left, that's responsible Christian stewardship.

Pay yourself. To help eliminate unnecessary stress, it is important to accrue savings. After you have paid your tithe, pay yourself. Savings must also become a discipline that you do before you pay any bills as you learn to live on "enough." Whether you save five percent or 20 percent, it is important to save something, and live on the remaining amount.

Live within your means. How we use what God has given us is the key to an abundant Christian life. Remember, "Much is required from those to whom much is given, for their responsibility is greater" (Luke 12:48). Read 1 Timothy 6:6–10 and distinguish your family's "needs" from "wants." How much food, recreation, or clothing is "enough" in your home?

Step 4: *Incorporate relaxation techniques into your daily routine.*

We know personally that relaxation techniques help you to successfully manage stress and reduce the emotional, negative thoughts that can accompany busy lives. Not only do your heart rate and blood pressure decrease when you practice relaxation, but your breathing becomes even and deeper, helping to quiet your body during times of turmoil.

True relaxation involves more than just being still. You may not be relaxed sitting in front of the TV with its frantic pace. Some people may have a high level of tension in their bodies and minds even during sleep. An example would be those who toss and turn at night or who grind their teeth while asleep.

But relaxation is a skill that all people have the potential to develop. Some of us are naturally better at relaxing than others, but we can all learn to relax effectively. Much like learning to play the piano or tennis, becoming good at relaxation involves time, patience, and practice. Learning to relax deeply and effectively is a skill that develops gradually and cannot be rushed or hurried.

Don't be surprised if the relaxed feeling you achieve begins to fade and dissipate once you get up and return to your normal activities. Many people find that it is only after several weeks of daily, consistent practice that they are able to maintain the relaxed feeling beyond the practice session itself.

Practice the relaxation response. The relaxation response is brought on by developing an inner quiet and peacefulness, a calming of negative thoughts and worries, and a mental focus away from the source of stress. This is a physiological state characterized by a feeling of warmth and quiet mental alertness, which is the opposite of the fight-or-flight response. When you learn the relaxation response, blood flow to the brain increases and brain waves shift from an alert *beta* rhythm to a relaxed *alpha* rhythm.

To learn the relaxation response, try the following steps:

- Set aside a period of about twenty minutes each day with your partner that you can devote to relaxation practice. This can be in the morning, afternoon, or evening; just pick a time when you may have few obligations or com-

mitments so you won't feel hurried or rushed. It is important to try to do the relaxation response together. We have
found that when both partners are relaxed after busy days
and can let their guard down, they will experience greater
intimacy.

- Remove outside distractions that can disrupt your concentration: turn off the radio, the television, even the ringer
on the telephone, if need be. During practice, it is important to either lie flat or recline comfortably so that your
whole body is supported, relieving as much tension or
tightness in your muscles as you can. This is difficult to do
upright, since your muscles must be tightened to maintain
the position. You can use a pillow or cushion under your
head, if this helps.

- Picture your body at peace. During the twenty-minute period, remain as still as possible; try to direct your thoughts
away from the events of the day. Focus your thoughts on
the immediate moment, and eliminate any outside
thoughts that may compete for your attention. Try to focus
on the different feelings or sensations you may notice
throughout your body. Notice which parts of your body
feel relaxed and loose and which parts feel tense and up-
tight. Some people find it helpful to repeat a word, such as
"Jesus," "love," or "peace," while doing this to keep their
mind from drifting.

- As you go through these steps, imagine every muscle in
your body becoming loose, relaxed, and free of any excess
tension. Picture all of your muscles beginning to unwind;
imagine them going loose and limp. Concentrate on
breathing slowly and evenly. Each time you exhale, picture
your muscles becoming even more relaxed, as if with each
breath you somehow breathe the tension away.

- At the end of twenty minutes, take a few moments to focus
on the feelings and sensations you have been able to
achieve. Notice whether areas that felt tense at first now
feel more relaxed and whether any areas of tension remain.

- Try progressive muscle relaxation (tensing and releasing each part of the body to circumvent the release of stress hormones that increase tension) as you do the relaxation response. Start with your feet and toes and tense these to the count of five, then release the tension. Continue up your body with your calves, knees, thighs, and so on.

If it seems hard to relax or if you need to learn about an individual approach for relaxation and stress management, it would be a good idea to see a clinical psychologist who specializes in working with these problems.

Week Six: De-Stress Your Life

Focus: Stress can show itself through a wide variety of physical changes and emotional responses. Stress symptoms vary greatly from one person to the next, and learning to identify the ways in which your body and mind show stress is the first step in "managing the self" and reducing external demands and pressures, as well as those that we place on ourselves.

Central Bible Truth: "Be still, and know that I am God" (Psalm 46:10, RSV).

Monday: *Take an inventory of life's stressors.*

Look at the Stress Warning Signals on pages 152–153, then do an inventory of the stressors in your daily life. What makes you cringe just thinking about it? For some people, it is fighting traffic on the way to work or a phone that won't quit ringing. Others tell of loathing long lines at the grocery store or not having enough money to pay bills.

Reflection and response:

Write down the specific things that cause stress for you and your partner. What are the barriers in your life that make time management more difficult? (Examples may be dealing with small children, too many bills, working different shifts, demanding careers.)

His: _____

_____

Hers: _____

_____

Tuesday: *Identify solutions for dealing with stress.*

No matter what the source of stress in your life, if it is not handled correctly it can disrupt any chance you might have had for intimacy. Take your list from Monday and try to identify creative solutions for dealing with each stressor so it does not take away from your relationship. For example, if a daily stressor for your spouse is that time of day when everyone comes home from school and work for dinner, think of ways to make this busy time more tolerant. Some suggestions might include directing the children out of doors to work on a project, or trying to talk with the children about taking a time-out to their rooms to give your spouse a reprieve. What other suggestions can you think of as you de-stress your life and increase emotional connectedness?

Remember: Stress can be controlled, but you have to make an effort by learning some workable techniques.

Stress-Reduction Plan

Set goals to reduce stress (see page 154 for sample):

1. _____

_____

_____

2. _____

_____

_____

3. _____

_____

_____

4. _____

_____

_____

5. _____

_____

_____

Discuss possible actions to overcome stress:

1. _____

_____

_____

2. _____

_____

_____

3. _____

_____

_____

4. _____

_____

_____

5. _____

_____

_____

Wednesday: *Learn to relax.*

Author M. Scott Peck, M.D., has said that in loving ourselves—that is, nurturing ourselves for the purpose of spiritual growth—we need to provide ourselves with all kinds of things that are not directly spiritual. To nourish the body, the spirit must be nourished. We need food and shelter. No matter how dedicated we are to spiritual nourishment, we also need rest and relaxation, exercise and distraction. Saints must sleep and prophets must play.[9]

Music has been proven to be an effective, non-pharmacologic approach to assist in reducing fear, anxiety, stress, or grief in chronically ill patients. It is just beginning to make its mark as a way to reduce stress, yet many are already reporting music therapy as the best way to lower stress.

While this may sound too easy to work, studies show that many of the sensations arising from music and pain are processed in the same areas of the brain. These areas are also responsible for coordinating our emotional responses. So, by focusing on and responding to music, we can relax, thus lending ourselves to greater intimacy with our partner. With this relaxation, we can decrease muscle tension and increase blood levels of endorphins. While our daily stressors don't go away, having less tension and anxiety can make them tolerable.[10]

For relaxation times with your partner, the pace of the music you choose should be slightly slower than your heart rate or approximately sixty beats a minute. This rhythm encourages your heart rate to slow down, and some studies of late have shown that this will also lower blood pressure. Composers such as Vivaldi and Chopin have works which would fit this category. We enjoy listening to organ recordings of great hymns and choral works, such as Handel's *Messiah*.

Reflection and response:

Begin the relaxation response as outlined on pages 158–160 with your partner today. Then try doing this while listening to relaxing music. Write down how you feel before doing this, then how you feel afterward. Were these techniques helpful in diminishing the tension and anxiety in your minds and bodies?

His:

Before: After:

_____   _____

_____   _____

_____   _____

_____   _____

Hers:

Before: After:

_____   _____

_____   _____

_____   _____

_____   _____

Thursday: *Focus on burnout.*

As you cut back your commitments and focus on what is most important in life, talk about burnout with each other. This is a state of physical, emotional, and mental exhaustion caused by illusory or impossible goals. Idealistic perfectionists are particularly vulnerable. They put themselves on a track that leads to burnout.

First they go through the honeymoon period, when a new job or commitment might seem wonderful. Next, they realize their initial expectations were unrealistic, and that leads to brownout, when enthusiasm and energy gives way to chronic fatigue and irritability. In full-scale burnout, life seems pointless and they have little hope for the future.[11]

Reflection and response:

What are your expectations about your marriage? Your family? Your career? Your outside commitments? While you have no control over life's interruptions, there are some things you do have control over, and one of the most effective ways to cope with stress is to change the way you treat yourself— your daily commitments, your exercise and activity level, and the way you spend any "downtime."

Write down some positive ways you can revamp your expectations to reduce stress in your lives:

His: _____

_____

Hers: _____

_____

Friday: *Find a circle of quiet.*

Jesus told the disciples, "Come with me by yourselves to a quiet place and get some rest." This is an important tool we can use today, because rest is a safety valve to use when pressured.

Reflection and response:

Find a quiet place with your partner today—away from the telephone, children, or other diversions. Review your journal entries and talk about the busyness of your lives. Do you see a pattern in your day? Are you more involved in career than family? Do you balance giving to the children with giving to your partner? What about spending time on spiritual disciplines—prayer, Bible study, fellowship with other Christians, worship?

Think of some positive changes you can make to revamp your time, allowing for more intimacy and less hurriedness? Write down ways you can do this:

His: _____

_____

Hers: _____

_____

Saturday: *Work on budget issues.*

We know personally that nothing is more exasperating than to have more bills than money at the end of the month. But we also know the inner peace that can be experienced when we are accountable to God in all areas of life, including the way we spend our money.

Reflection and response:

Talk openly today about your financial situation. What stumbling blocks do you have? List these. How do you see your marriage affected by budgeting problems? Talk about this. Make goals together to get in control of budget issues so that your relationship does not undergo unnecessary stress.

His: _____

_____

Hers: _____

_____

Sunday: *Reach out to others.*

Because cocooning is the tendency for most of us after a busy week, make plans today to get together with another couple for a social outing. This may be to go out to dinner or to get a quick lunch after church.

Reflection and response:

As you break your habit of soothing stress with cocooning and begin to socialize with others, you are helping your health and well-being. Think of socialization as not only good for the mind and spirit, but as immunization against disease.

Write here how you felt before you went out with another couple. How did you feel afterward?

His: _____

_____

Hers: _____

_____

7

WEEK SEVEN

Get Up and Get Moving

When we suggested that Ginah and Ray get into a daily exercise program to enhance intimacy in their marriage, they couldn't believe us. "Who's ever heard of using exercise to boost intimacy?" they questioned.

Perhaps it does sound questionable that walking, playing tennis, or riding bikes together can increase the emotional connectedness in your marriage, but we are among many who have found regular exercise to do just that. While it is a well-known fact that exercise promotes good health, combats the risk of disease by lowering blood pressure, cholesterol levels, and body fat, and overall enhances the quality of one's life, we have found that by improving our physical fitness, we can boost our emotional and marital fitness as well.

Unfortunately, most people—married or not—do not exercise on a regular basis. Government statistics show that 60 percent of all Americans get no regular exercise, and that about one-third of all American adults are obese, a statistic that has remained steady in the last two decades. Additionally, about $5.7 billion is spent each year in the United States in medical expenses and lost productivity of people who could have fought off heart disease with a little exercise. Compare this with the $30 billion spent on diet foods and diet programs each year by the American public. Somewhere, we have missed the point and are paying for it with our income, our health, and our relationships with others.

According to the Centers for Disease Control and Prevention (CDC), 56 percent of men and 44 percent of women between ages 18 and 29 exercise regularly. But these numbers drop to 44 percent and 40 percent, respectively, among people 30 to 44.

Exploration:

- How much do you exercise each week? Your partner?
- Did you exercise regularly when you first met? In early marriage years?
- What holds you back from participating in a daily exercise program? (work, no time, no energy, children, laziness, physical limitations)

There's No Excuse

Lydia told us that she and her husband, Bill, could get on an exercise program . . . if only they had some energy. "When we get home after working and try to meet the kids' needs, there is no energy left for each other, much less for exercise," Lydia shared honestly.

Cameron and Kim, the new parents of twins, felt that exercise would help them feel better and have time out to talk, but they had no one to keep their infants. "We'd love to get out and get back in shape," Cameron said. "But with no family in town, what would we do with the twins?"

Inez and her husband, Walter, both shook their heads when we suggested getting into a daily walking routine. "We are too old to do anything like that," they said skeptically. "Walt has an arthritic knee, so we try to avoid activity."

You deserve to know that the more you increase your exercise and activity level, the more energy you will have. At one point in our marriage, we too believed that we did not have the energy to go and "work it out." However, we discovered that the "happy hormones" or the elevated endorphins that resulted from activity made us feel better about life and each other. They increased our self-esteem as well as helped to relieve anxiety, and the good news is that they are absolutely free—if you get up and get moving!

Exercise is also beneficial in reducing stress, and as we discussed in Chapter 6, this is particularly important today when couples are too harried from long hours at work and family demands to react calmly. This stress reduction provides an added benefit as you can cope with life's interruptions in a reasonable manner.

You may be wondering how exercise reduces stress. Not only does physical activity increase *alpha* waves that are associated with relaxation and meditation, exercise also acts as a displacement defense mechanism. How does this work? You may get up early each day to deal with careers and children, then after working hard all day, not get into bed until late at night. This ongoing daily stress and lack of healthful sleep might cause you to become more irritable and quick-tempered around your partner.

But exercise can help. Most studies now show that exercise can help direct the anxiety and emotions away and help you gain some hopeful feelings about yourself and your relationship. If you have ever participated in a lengthy period of aerobics or walked for several miles, perhaps you know the benefit of this displacement defense mechanism. Isn't it difficult to worry about daily stresses or even relationship battles when you are working hard physically? All that is on your mind is getting through the routine . . . not the problems you face each day.

Fred and Mary tell of realizing this extra benefit of exercise. After their youngest child started college three years ago, their relationship seemed to be at a standstill. "Fred was busy with his business and worked long hours during the week," Mary shared. "When he came home, he would head toward the den, eat his dinner on a TV tray; then the only exercise he got was channel surfing while dozing in his recliner. We had no life together.

"Then his business began to fail," Mary continued. "Insurance problems created a real struggle for his cash flow, and we worried that Becky might have to come home from college. Instead of talking about the problems, Fred stared at the TV, unapproachable to me, or anyone, for that matter."

Fred and Mary began a regular exercise program after his physician told him that the stress of a failing business was compromising his health. It was only a few months before they received an added bonus—increased intimacy in their marriage.

"The first few times we walked, we did so in silence," Fred interjected. "But after that week, we began to look forward to walking together each night and talking about our days. I poured my heart out about the concerns with the business, and Mary offered to come work with me to help get through the crunch. Now we both feel better, and we feel closer. We are learning to understand each other—something we've never really worked at."

Not only does exercise provide an opportunity to be together and converse as Fred and Mary experienced, it also restores the body's neurochemical balance, which in turn affects our emotional state. Several studies performed on groups of women have reported dramatic increases in sexual activity and arousal after beginning a regular exercise program. Not only were they more physically fit, but their stress levels were greatly reduced, helping to enhance their sex life.

Exercise is today's legal wonder drug that definitely improves your mood and lowers stress. While for some of us, exercise and weight control are already an important part of our busy, health-conscious lifestyle, the reality is that many of us have ignored these disciplines—disciplines that can increase your personal well-being as well as your marital satisfaction.

You may be saying, "But we don't have time to exercise." Or, "We don't have a baby-sitter to allow us to go out together." Or even, "If you had to live our busy schedules, you'd know what we meant." No matter what your age, how busy you are, or if you have access to sitters or not, you can incorporate a regular exercise routine into your daily lives.

Steps to Getting Up and Getting Moving

Perhaps the greatest benefit exercise gives is that it diminishes tension by reducing stress. While there are many factors that allow us to cope with stress, researchers have found that a person's emotional and mental state is important. It is believed that positive thoughts, feeling relaxed, and a general sense of well-being can lower the overall stressed feeling, anxiety, and irritability. Recent studies have revealed what we all have thought to be true: exercise is one of the most effective mood-regulating behaviors, and the best general strategy to change a bad mood is a combination of relaxation, stress management, cognitive, and exercise techniques.

Step 1: *Make the commitment.*

While you may agree that exercise is beneficial, many people feel that conditioning is for the young. But studies show that everyone—even senior citizens—can benefit greatly from movement and exercise. One study tested a group of 100 frail nursing-home patients over a period of time. Those who received exercise training increased muscle strength and gait velocity; their ability to climb stairs improved. Those patients who did not receive exercise training remained the same or declined in strength. This study concluded that even the frail elderly greatly benefit from exercise as a means to counteract muscle weakness and physical frailty. If the frail elderly can show physical improvement from exercise, imagine what exercise will do for you!

Step 2: *Make time each day to exercise.*

Finding the time to exercise may seem more difficult than actually performing the activity, but once you and your partner begin an activity and exercise program, you will be surprised how you will depend on this time of movement and activity. You will find your overall performance improves in every area of your life—career, child-rearing, relationships with other people, and relationships with each other. Some couples we know even tell of adding another day of exercise on their "day off" because they enjoy the boost of endorphins, the body's natural pain relievers, from aerobic training.

It takes time to get a routine established. While an ongoing, daily exercise program will help you to see some short-term results of improved mood, it takes weeks to months to really catch the benefit of weight control and greater energy.

Go slowly at first, then build as you are able. Starting small, then building into a full exercise program will let you become adjusted to the exercise and help you to make it a habit. For example, if you are healthy adults and start out walking and swimming as your exercise, start with just ten minutes a day the first week. As you increase in strength and endurance, add five minutes the second week, then another five minutes the third week, and so on until you get up to an acceptable program.

A word of caution: If you have not been physically active,

be sure to get your physician's consent before starting any exercise program.

Step 3: *Do what you enjoy.*

The number one fitness activity in America is walking. Not only can you do this anywhere, you don't need special equipment or clothes to get out and exercise. We enjoy walking together, whether around the neighborhood or on the beach after an early dinner out. Deb's parents, who are recently retired, enjoy riding bicycles together and have made this physical activity part of their daily routine, clocking over five miles per day on neighborhood streets. Another couple, Fred and Mary, tell of exercising indoors with two stationary bicycles because of their work schedules. All of us witness to feeling less anxiety and tension in our marriages and in the way we handle life's interruptions.

The most important factor to consider when developing an exercise and activity program with your partner is to choose activities that you enjoy and do these activities in moderation— both in amount and intensity. One main reason people drop exercise programs is that they get bored; either the exercise becomes too mundane, the scenery is too repetitious, or the results are not startling enough to keep them motivated. Another reason people quit exercising is that they try to do too much, too soon, and instead of receiving aerobic benefits, they are injured.

Exploration:

What exercises do you enjoy? Make a list together of the exercises and activities that you enjoy. (Some examples might be biking, golf, hiking, rowing, running, swimming, tennis, or walking.)

Step 4: *Learn to keep track of your pulse.*

To check your target heart rate zone, take your pulse periodically. You can find a pulse by placing your finger (not your thumb) on the artery on the side of your windpipe (your carotid pulse) or on the thumb side of the wrist. Stop periodically during your workout and count your pulse rate for ten seconds. Multiply this number by six to get your total pulse for one minute.

Your target heart rate zone will vary depending on your age and your fitness level. To compute your heart rate zone, subtract your age from 220 and multiply this number by 60 percent. This gives you the low range. Now subtract your age from 220 and multiply this number by 80 percent to get your high range.

It is important to keep your heart rate in this zone while exercising.

Sample Target Heart Rate Zone for Age 45

Low zone: $220-45=175\times60\%=105$
High zone: $220-45=175\times80\%=140$

Stay on Target With Fitness

Use the following chart to guide you in finding your estimated target heart rate as you stay within the training range:

Age	Low	High	Age	Low	High
20–21	120	162	54–55	102	132
22–25	114	156	56–59	96	132
26–27	114	156	60–62	96	126
28–29	114	156	63–65	96	126
30–35	114	150	66	90	126
36	108	150	67–70	90	120
37–44	108	144	71–74	90	120
45	108	138	75	90	114
46–51	102	138	76–78	84	114
52–53	102	132			

Step 5: *Make exercise part of your daily routine.*

While most studies state that forty-five consecutive minutes of conditioning exercise is necessary to get a cardiovascular benefit, there are some new studies that say the daily workout does not have to be done all at the same time. These studies report that you can get the same benefit from ten-minute segments of exercise, three to four times a day, as you do from forty-five consecutive minutes.

Jim and Paula told of working out in short bouts throughout the day, taking walks before work and after dinner with their two young children. For some people, working out in segments allows them to fit their exercise program in on workdays. Like Jim and Paula, you and your spouse could walk ten minutes before work, do two ten-minute segments of walking at the office during your coffee break, then walk fifteen minutes in the evening. And it does not all have to be walking. As we stated previously, depending on your exercise preference, you could alternate your conditioning exercises (or cross train), such as stepping before work, walking at work, then swimming after work.

If you are very sedentary and have great resistance to following a daily program as recommended, then adding segments (ten to fifteen minutes at a time) of exercise may help motivate you to begin a regular program. You would have to become disciplined to work out in segments, such as taking the stairs instead of an elevator, parking at the end of the parking lot while shopping, walking to work (or partway), walking to the grocery store, raking leaves, actively cleaning your house (mopping, vacuuming, scrubbing), and more.

Week Seven: Get Up and Get Moving

Synopsis: As stated, exercise is believed to increase the secretion of endorphins in the brain. This naturally produced substance has been called the body's own opiate and gives a narcotic effect, inducing a feeling of happiness, peacefulness, and tranquillity. There have been many studies done to show that exercise, along with the boosted endorphin levels, really does boost confidence and self-esteem and reduce tension, anxiety, and depression—all important factors for increasing intimacy in a relationship.

Central Bible Truth: "Haven't you yet learned that your body is the home of the Holy Spirit God gave you, and that he lives within you? Your own body does not belong to you" (1 Corinthians 6:19).

Monday: *Make time to play again.*

Have you ever taken time to follow your child around while he is playing? Children laugh, sing, climb, run, skip, and embrace life to the fullest as they engage in active play. Compare a child's playtime with an adult's playtime. For many of us, when we have leisure time, we spend it lying on the couch or snoozing in bed. But activity and exercise are important to adults as these help inoculate us against stress and its symptoms.

Reflection and response:

Write down the five activities you enjoyed as a child (biking, running, jumping rope, swinging, climbing, sliding, among many). Pick one of these activities to do with your spouse today. You may need to go to a nearby playground to take advantage of the equipment. Write down how you feel before and after the play activity.

His: _____

_____

Hers: _____

_____

Tuesday: *Set personal and marital goals.*

Getting motivated to begin an exercise program is not easy. Studies show that of those people who do begin an exercise program, more than 50 percent drop out within six months. But goal setting can enable you and your partner to budget exercise time, just as you would your finances, setting aside a period of planned time each day for activity and movement.

It is important to remember your personal abilities when exercising. If you have a specific health condition such as arthritis or a heart problem, ask your doctor for a reference to specialized exercise programs. Check with you local YMCA, the Arthritis Foundation, or the Heart Association, depending on your need.

Reflection and response:

Goals are vital for success in anything we do. With an exercise program, setting goals will help turn your initial enthusiasm into a reality. But without specific goals, you have no way to measure growth. Make sure that the goals you set are specific, and write these down so you will visualize the commitment. Also make sure that the goals are realistic as you attempt something you can actually achieve. Review these goals frequently and make changes as necessary.

Suggested exercise goals:

1. To exercise at least four to five days a week with my partner.

2. To start slowly and make this a lifetime of health and conditioning.

3. To plan this exercise time in our daily schedule.

Outline a personal fitness plan that you can do with your spouse, including walking, aerobics, or other exercise, and post this plan on the refrigerator as a reminder. Make a list of the pros and cons of exercise versus not exercising, and write down your personal and marital exercise goals here:

His:

1. _____

2. _____

3. _____

Hers:

1. _____

2. _____

3. _____

Wednesday: *Get up and get moving.*

Brush the dust off those running shoes (the ones hidden in the back of your closet!) and put your "feet to pavement." Start slowly with just twenty minutes a day, and checkmark those days that you follow through. Studies show that it takes twenty-one days to make any change in behavior become a habit, so don't give up.

Reflection and response:

Exercise and activity should bring enjoyment to your life as you focus on pleasurable activities, such as gardening, taking a walk and gathering flowers along the way, rather than the push for muscle and weight loss. After you exercise with your spouse, write down your feelings, both positive and negative. Knowing that your body is the temple of the Holy Spirit, does this make a difference in your motivation to care for yourself?

His: _____

_____

Hers: _____

_____

Thursday: *Incorporate activity as exercise.*

The key to sticking with any type of exercise program is diversity and listening to your body. Going full force this week will not make up for years of ignoring physical activity. You can burn 100 calories a mile, whether you walk it or run it, so moderation is important.

Reflection and response:

Turn to activity today instead of doing your regular exercise routine. Plan a picnic in the park, then ride your bikes to the destination, and spend time hiking or even playing on the playground equipment together. Write down any new impressions you have of your spouse as you spend active time together.

His: _____

Hers: _____

Friday: *Be prepared for motivation lapses.*

Reaching your goals with exercise and relaxation may require repeated attempts, but perseverance is the key. As you begin your program try to stay focused on your goal even when obstacles occur—and they will occur. How can you do this?

- Believe in yourself and your fitness goals.
- Take responsibility for yourself.
- Launch out toward your goal and your "feelings" will follow.
- Imagine how wonderful you are going to feel when you get fully into your exercise and relaxation program.
- See this as an opportunity of a lifetime.

It's all up to you. If you think you can succeed with your exercise plan, then you can. If you think this plan is setting you up for another failure in your exercise journey, it probably will.

Reflection and response:

If you believe you can make a three-week commitment, do so. Then reevaluate your commitment and go another three weeks. If you feel that this plan could work for six months, a year, five years, or even a lifetime, then take that leap of faith and launch into an exercise program with your whole being.

Remember, start slowly. Allow yourself to be human and realize that sometimes you will not feel like exercising. See these lapses as growth experiences, continue to keep your exercise journal, and move toward your goal of decreased stress and anxiety and increased intimacy in your marriage.

Write your exercise and activity goals here:

His: _____

_____

Hers: _____

_____

Saturday: *Celebrate health and wellness.*

Keep in mind that your exercise and activity program is a lifetime commitment. A number of large, lengthy studies have shown that people who exercise regularly live longer. For example, researchers from the Cooper Institute for Aerobics Research in Dallas gauged fitness in about 13,000 men and women by measuring how long the volunteers could exercise on a treadmill. Then the researchers followed them for an average of more than eight years. As fitness increased, the death rate fell. But by far the biggest drop in mortality—60 percent for the men, nearly 50 percent for the women—occurred between the most unfit volunteers and those who were just slightly more fit.[1]

Reflection and response:

Review your week and write down the successes you had with exercise and activity. Also write down the obstacles you encountered. Finally, make a commitment to continue this program and put this in writing:

His: _____

_____

Hers: _____

_____

Sunday: *Renew your commitment to spiritual exercise.*

You have been on your Intimate Journey for seven weeks. How have your attitudes changed toward each other? Have you made new discoveries about yourself? Your spouse?

Reflection and response:

Write some of the challenges you face in your marriage, such as coping with personal illness, job dissatisfactions, or problems raising children. Pray about these challenges and ask God to guide you in discovering his will for your life and marriage. Have you made any new discoveries about yourself? Your partner? Your relationship with Christ Jesus?

Write down the new discoveries you have made:

His: _____

_____

_____

_____

Hers: _____

_____

_____

_____

8

WEEK EIGHT

Don't Let Your Family Fade the Heat

Now that you have progressed through seven weeks of your Intimate Journey, have you considered what the greatest challenge is for you and your partner that blocks intimacy in your marriage? Raising children in a hurried society? Caring for aging parents? Staying on top of an upwardly mobile career? Trying to meet the demands of volunteer commitments?

Perhaps the greatest challenge married couples face is learning to take time for themselves while juggling kids, in-laws, careers, and commitments. While we gave suggestions in how to effectively manage time in Week Five, it is often difficult when you have many family members making constant demands. In fact, many of us agree with Betty, a high school English teacher, mother of three, and president of the parent organization at an elementary school, when she says, "I can be having a great day at school, feeling totally relaxed and in control. When I get home, one little thing can go wrong, and I go crazy. The least interruption makes me stressed, and that blocks any chance of intimacy in our marriage."

Betty's not alone. The stress of juggling too many outside commitments along with household chores and meeting family needs affects so many couples today that most of us feel as if we are in constant overdrive twenty-four hours a day, even as we sleep . . . IF we sleep. Martin, a thirty-six-year-old successful business owner, father and Little League coach, tells of feeling constant tension in his life: "When I walk in our home from work, my anxiety level triples. I start to think of all the things I need to do for my wife, kids, and baseball team as my next jobs as Honey, Dad, and Coach begin."

It has been said that Americans are often portrayed as being forever busy. Tradition has it that our reverence for the work ethic is second to none. According to this image, even our leisure moments are crammed with pressing duties and obligations; things are always unfinished or children are in need of our attention.[1] A recent poll revealed that although the number of hours Americans say they work actually increased by 20 percent in the past ten years, the number of leisure hours dropped by 32 percent.

Life certainly DOES NOT have to be this way . . . not if you take time to understand your right to have an intimate relationship with your mate, and stop letting your family fade the heat.

Parenthood: A Critical Period

Marie told us that with each child added to their household it seemed as though she and her husband drifted further apart, and what she is saying is very real. As the parents of three young adults, we remember the joy and excitement of bringing home each baby into the caring fold of our home. But we also remember the marital strain as our life as husband and wife was interrupted with new demands.

Studies show that relationship patterns between spouses

who become mother and father undergo great changes. In fact, parenthood represents a critical period in a family unit. Some new parents are confronted with drastic changes in finances along with caring for a new infant who is difficult or fussy. For those parents who already have young children at home, the new baby adds to the turmoil and tension already there.

When our friend Kate, the mother of two elementary-age boys and head nurse at a local hospital, called several months ago, she told us she wanted to run away—from everything. "Isn't there a home for overworked mothers?" she asked. "I work the early shift at a local hospital, so I am out of the house before the sun is up each morning. By the time I get off work, stop by the grocery store, and pick up the boys from Little League practice, it is nighttime. Some days I feel that if one more child makes a demand on me, I will leave. I cannot help it, but I feel emotionally and physically drained all the time."

What about you? Do you feel like running away as you juggle too many outside activities or a busy career along with rearing children? The pressures are overwhelming for most parents today. In the 1930s, less than 20 percent of women in the United States worked outside the home. Today, over 58 percent of the mothers with children under the age of six years leave to go to work each day. Added to the responsibility of raising children is another demand that is hitting the "sandwich" generation—caregiving to aging parents. With modern medicine prolonging life, most of us will need to face the responsibility of assisting our parents in the near future. And if what current research indicates is true, millions of Americans will spend more years caring for elderly parents than they do caring for their own children. A recent Congressional study showed that American women will spend seventeen years raising children and eighteen years caring for their parents. Add to this caregiving challenge the millions of American women who must also work outside the home, either full or part time, and then take care of dependent children and parents after hours.

Sandra, an energetic forty-nine-year-old woman, is a marketing consultant and also has her seventy-eight-year-old mother, an Alzheimer's patient, living in her home. Sandra chose to care for her mother and enjoyed having her in the home—until recently.

Last summer, her father-in-law was diagnosed with cancer. He underwent chemotherapy and radiation and is now recuperating at home with Sandra and her husband, Rick. "I feel like I'm being bounced back and forth with no hope of stopping," she told us. "I go from being a marketing consultant full of energy and ideas to a child and wife who feels like the entire world is sitting on my shoulders. I feel run down and know I'm depressed."

Sandra tells of going the extra mile in everything she does, but now she feels she can't do enough to please anyone, especially herself. "Intimacy in marriage? To be honest, Rick stays at work until late at night to avoid having to deal with these problems."

When Does the Turmoil End?

Sandra is not alone in coping with life's interruptions without support. In the past twenty years, couples have shared with us the following symptoms as they told of family interventions creating stumbling blocks in their marriages:

- We have no passion or emotional oneness since Dad moved in.
- She always rejects me when I try to get close and the kids are around.
- He turns away from me at night when we are in bed because our child's room is right next to ours.
- We never share deepest emotions or feelings because our family is so harried and out-of-control.
- He never affirms me as important even though I stay home to raise our children.
- We don't communicate because the kids are always around.

- She gets angry when I talk to her about disciplining the kids and blames me for not being in control.
- He holds a grudge from years ago when I quit my job to stay home and raise our children.
- She hates that we have to struggle since I vowed to help Mom and Dad with their retirement.
- The baby's crying really bothers him and has driven a wedge between us.
- She allows her family to take precedence over our marriage.
- She has not been romantic since the baby was born.
- We never go anywhere alone because she won't leave the kids.
- She always calls "Daddy" instead of taking my advice.
- He compares my cooking and homemaking to his mom's, and I always lose.
- Since my mother moved in with us, he does not come home from work until well after dark.
- She never kisses me anymore since her mother moved in with us.
- She spends all her time at night with the kids.
- He can't stand dealing with our teens and makes me do all the disciplining.
- He always watches television to avoid dealing with the children, and ignores me too.

Do any of these statements sound familiar? The interesting fact is that these symptoms were shared by men and women who have reasonably strong marriages, yet they have missed one key point: They have allowed their family to fade the heat.

Exploration:

- Do your family responsibilities interfere with intimacy in your marriage?
- List three symptoms of family intervention in your marriage:

1. _____

2. _____

3. _____

We're Lonely and Tired

One father of two, thirty-seven-year-old Ron, tells of wanting intimacy with his wife, Pam, but faces feelings of loneliness instead. "I've never felt so lonely as I do now," Ron confides. "Don't get me wrong, I love Pam. It just seems that with her new teaching job, car-pooling the kids to after-school activities, and now helping her retired parents, the spark between us is gone. When we finally crawl into bed late each night, it takes all of her energy to just mumble 'good-night.' Between the demands everyone makes and her attempt to meet these demands, we hardly know each other anymore."

Ron continues: "The sad part is that Pam used to be my best friend."

Although emotional involvement is a growing need for men and women today, most of us are faced with a grave problem. We have found that for many couples, it is difficult to cultivate an intimate relationship while trying to be perfect in other areas, whether the perfect adult child or parent, employee or employer, church or family member, neighbor or friend. And most people, like Josh, speak of being "too tired to care."

Josh, a husband of nineteen-years and father of three teenage daughters, told us, "After Pat and I work long days and come home to housework, homework, and kids, we barely have time for a quick kiss, much less talk about our feelings or sustain intimacy in our relationship."

We have personally experienced that what Josh claims is true. It is easy to put your marriage relationship on the back burner as you tend to career and family needs. And taking the marriage off this back-burner status or pulling back from outside obligations to put the relationship first often seems impossible.

"There are just too many obstacles, diversions, and expectations to get close anymore," one busy mother and teacher said. "We're so out of touch with each other's realities."

Mary Ellen, a thirty-six-year-old mother of two, is an excellent example of how intimacy in marriage is stifled when we try to meet our family's expectations. Her friends call her "Super Mom," and Mary Ellen fits the bill. She leads a community Bible study group each week, volunteers to run the school's clinic for two-hours each morning, directs the church's cherub choir, spends every afternoon car-pooling her daughters to dancing school, then takes dinner to her elderly father each evening. "But Jack [her husband] and I never have time alone," she complains. "We hardly know each other anymore."

Let's face it. Aren't most of us like Mary Ellen as we benevolently seek to participate in life? Don't most of us put our personal needs, including intimacy, as a low priority on our list, hoping that someday we will get our marriages off the back-burner status and pick up where we left off? The problem with this is that as you grow in years, you will also be confronted with more and more interruptions—serious interruptions, such as personal illness or the illness of your partner, death of friends and loved ones, loss of income, and more. If your marriage is not emotionally bonded, it will be difficult to pull together when life's emergencies hit.

Watch for Symptoms of Burnout

If being a parent or caregiver to elderly family members is overwhelming, leaving you tired and drained of enthusiasm, you may be experiencing the pain of burnout. This is a state of physical and emotional exhaustion that is quite common among caretakers, persons who are constantly nurturing others.

Ministers, nurses, physicians, social workers, and, yes, caring parents and caregivers are usually the victims of burnout.

Typical Symptoms of Burnout

- negative and rigid attitudes
- dread of starting a new day
- difficulty in sleeping
- irritability and bursts of anger
- lack of energy or enthusiasm
- feelings of being overwhelmed

People who are suffering from various stages of burnout, have similar warning signs from stress, such as rapid heartbeat, stomachache, headache, or back pain. But before these symptoms signal that your body is under pressure, learn to make time to evaluate your obligations and pace yourself.

Steps to Stopping Your Family From Fading the Heat

Putting yourself and your marriage relationship as priorities in life will help you take better care of your children, your parents, and others. Let's look at ways this can be done.

Step 1: *Prevent burnout.*

Verbalize your feelings. It is important to first understand your feelings, then verbalize them in order to put yourself as a priority in life. Talk about the pressures of being a parent or caregiver with your mate or trusted friend. Nothing can be clearly understood without open discussion. Realize that negative feelings are normal and okay; no relationship is free from resentment or anger.

John, an insurance executive, father of three teens, and caregiver to his parents, told of finding it necessary to identify his emotions and find out what was triggering his anger so he didn't explode at home: "If a family member has been slack in fulfilling his responsibility, I try to talk it out before resentment builds. Once I identify the initial cause of anger, anxiety, or even resentment, I can begin to handle these feelings constructively without hurting anyone."

Set worthy goals. Goal setting is vital in avoiding and overcoming parent or caregiving burnout. Because of society's pressures, we may try to become "Super Man" or "Wonder Woman." We overheard several women talking at a local school meeting, and each seemed to outdo the other with claims of having the "perfect" child. Many parents feel pressed to compete with everyone for the most talented, brightest, and socially adjusted child. Yet, in the midst of trying to seek excellence in parenting, we need to set priorities in our use of time and set realistic goals that make a difference. Is spending time together away from family members a priority in our marriage, or is a popular TV show occupying that time? Are evenings out without the children a regular commitment, or do we find ourselves too tired to celebrate our marriage relationship after caring for family members all day?

Parents and caregivers must prioritize their goals, and in doing so, they will find lesser activities not as important. The main priority in the lives of Christian couples must be God, our relationships, and our families. Only then will our marriages begin to experience an inner peace that can help heal burnout.

Care for your own needs. To remember that one is a person first, a wife or husband second, then a parent or caregiver third is also important in curing burnout. We cheat everyone, including ourselves, if we ignore our personal needs. We have been given the Great Commandment in the Gospels: "You must love others as much as yourself" (Mark 12:31). This verse presupposes that we love ourselves.

If you are experiencing a nagging feeling of emptiness and loneliness that often accompanies parenting or caregiving burnout, be sure to reread Chapter 5 and learn how to set priorities in your life. Also make plans to revitalize your personal faith with a specific schedule for Bible study, prayer, and quiet time that lets you boost your personal strengths to cope with a demanding family life. Post this schedule, and checkmark the days you follow through as you learn to take time out for yourself.

Learn to be "good enough." Good enough is a term we all must become familiar with as we try to balance the many commitments in our lives. This means that sometimes we must block family responsibilities from interfering with the intimacy in our marriage as we learn to maintain balance. When a child begins to demand more from you and your mate than you can reasonably give, feelings of guilt can take over.

You can learn how to block out time for yourself so that you are a "good enough" husband or wife, parent, and adult child. Edward Hale states the importance of realizing that we are only one person in his poem "Lend a Hand."

I am only one,
But still I am one.
I cannot do everything,
But still I can do something.
And because I cannot do everything
I will not refuse to do the something
that I can do.

This is the attitude men and women must take as they care for those in the family along with caring for their relationship together. We can do the best possible or be "good enough," but we also have to know that we cannot attempt to do everything without hurting ourselves and our relationships.

Lou, a mother of three and caregiver to her aging parents, told how she found herself resenting the daily annoyances that occur with her children. "After being up all night with Mom, anything the kids did got on my nerves. I finally got some help at home, which gave me a break during the day. I realized that when I was rested and my spirit was at peace, I was a better mother, caregiver, and wife to Jake."

If we are full of personal tensions and anxieties, perhaps we are not loving ourselves enough. Unless we care for ourselves as Lou did, we may not be adequate to love and care for our partner.

Use baby-sitters. Baby-sitters can take over when the pressures of parenting begin to overwhelm us. When our three children were young, we were blessed with an older couple from our church who served as surrogate grandparents. This couple had no grandchildren and enjoyed coming to our home while we went out. We felt confident that our children were being loved and cared for.

A young teen may help you as a "mother's helper," coming to care for your children so you can take a nap or read a book. Remember, when you are well-rested, all relationships improve. An older teen can baby-sit and give you a chance to go for a walk or go shopping. Interview these sitters and make sure their values and methods of discipline are appropriate. Then keep their telephone numbers handy and use them often before the role of "parent" becomes overwhelming.

Seek respite care. This is care given to aging parents while you are away. It could be for a few hours or all day, depending on the need. This person would stay with your parent and be the responsible caregiver in your absence, making necessary decisions as directed. Many churches are actively involved in this volunteer service.

Step 2: *Divide home responsibilities.*

There are more than fourteen million working married couples with children (under the age of eighteen) in the United States, according to the U.S. Census Bureau. The ongoing stress of just trying to make ends meet—by both husbands and wives—makes it imperative that all family members share the work load at home; yes, both sexes can fold clothes and mow lawns!

For women only: Today's woman has more opportunities than ever before as the possibilities of careers are only limited by our dreams and education. In the midst of these opportunities, women can still be mothers, giving birth to children and nurturing them into responsible adulthood. The problem arises as women go into the work force, whether because of financial need or personal desire, yet are expected to maintain the role of the traditional mom. How can we do it all? Studies show that women still do 80 percent of the housework whether they are employed or not. When responsibilities become too demanding with working, raising children, and maintaining a home, something will give, and that something is usually intimacy in marriage.

While our society is accepting of the new role of women in the work force, it is not so willing to alter the role of "perfect wife, mother, and homemaker." This adds to the frantic fast track that we find ourselves on daily. It is supposed that the woman who is not overworked does not take herself or her job seriously. This is a misconception. We do not have to work ourselves into being accepted. We have to learn to accept ourselves and do what we can to be a "good enough" person, wife, mother, or career woman. Allowing ourselves to stay on the fast track with no reprieve creates physical and psychological problems.

The fast track is just that, a fast track. It feels that way; it affects your family that way. Some women can do truckloads of work and not feel stressed or intrude on their family relationships. Others may only do half as much and not cope well with that. Only you can decide if your daily load needs adjustment. If you are short and irritable with your spouse and family, you feel that they get in the way of your completing your tasks and goals, it may be time to rethink your priorities.[2]

As working parents, we have a fair division of home chores between our five family members—all able-bodied individuals—for we have experienced that if one person constantly does all the household chores, there is going to be resentment. By letting children help with home responsibilities, parents have more time for personal care and building an intimate relationship with each other. The added bonus is that children need to feel "needed" in the family. While your child will not admit that setting the table each night boosts his self-esteem, it does give him a strong feeling of importance in the family unit.

Post the "Home Rules." In our home, we have the following "Home Rules" posted on our refrigerator as representation of Mom and Dad's position on responsibility in the family. You might copy these, discuss them with family members, and post them in your home.

Home Rules

If you sleep on it . . . make it up.
If you wear it . . . hang it up.
If you drop it . . . pick it up.
If you eat out of it . . . put it in the sink
(or dishwasher).

> If you step on it . . . wipe it off.
> If you open it . . . close it.
> If you empty it . . . fill it up.
> If it rings . . . answer it.
> If it howls . . . feed it.
> If it cries . . . love it.[3]

Set reasonable goals. Outline a list of the household responsibilities that need to be accomplished daily, weekly, monthly, and semi-annually with your partner. Your list might include:

Daily	Weekly	Monthly	Semi-Annually
cooking	vacuuming	cleaning	organizing
washing	mopping	windows	closets
dishes	floors	heavy	major cleanup
laundry	changing	yardwork	painting
cleaning	sheets	cleaning	pressure
bathrooms	dusting	gutters	washing
		trimming	
		hedges	

After you have made your list of all household and yard responsibilities, also come up with a strategy for getting these jobs done, using all family members as active participants and putting initials by each responsibility, such as:

Daily	Weekly	Monthly	Semi-Annually
cooking (Mom)	vacuuming (B.B.)	cleaning windows (R.B)	organizing closets (All)
washing dishes(A.B.)	mopping floors (Dad)	heavy yardwork (All)	major cleanup (All)
laundry (All)	changing sheets (All)	cleaning gutters (Dad)	painting (R.B.)

cleaning	dusting (A.B.)	trimming	pressure
bathrooms		hedges (R.B.)	washing (Dad)
(B.B.)			

Be sure you respect each other's personal style, and don't look at any household chore as gender specific. In our family, Bob enjoys doing the laundry, and I (Deb) enjoy cooking and grocery shopping. You may also have to lower your standards a bit, depending on the age and ability of your children, but with some help and encouragement, they can learn to get the job done.

Delegate responsibilities. If you grew up in a traditional family where Dad worked long hours and Mom stayed home to "keep the house," you may not feel comfortable sitting down with your partner and dividing home responsibilities. But to alleviate the mounting pressure that occurs when you blend demanding careers along with raising families, all members must participate equally in household responsibilities.

After deciding which jobs must be done and when, write these on a large sheet of poster board. Let your children decide how the chores should be distributed, and make this a part of your daily and weekly routine. When our children first began helping in the home, we posted the list of chores and checked each off as the children completed them. Now that they are older, they know what needs to be done and take pride in doing it.

Our friend Jan devised a Job Jar that lets all family members choose chores each day. She writes down on paper the various household responsibilities for each day, then allows the first members up for the day to have first pick out of the jar. The benefit is that the jobs change, and the same person is not "stuck" with doing the same job each day.

Remember, as parents our most important duty is to train our children to be self-sufficient—not to treat them as invited guests in their own home. We need to learn to enjoy the special attributes of each of our children, but to also draw the line and make sure they are active and equal participants in the family.

Work as a team. Recent studies show that 71 percent of families feel stressed at least some of the time. With two parents working outside the home, 40 percent say they have job-related conflicts. We have experienced that teamwork is vital for sharing the load at home and dealing with the stresses that come from raising children and caring for other family members. But to be a team, you have to act like one before life's interruptions hit. You see, a team has one goal or purpose. The members work toward the goal together, each supporting the other. If they come up against a problem, they problem solve and tackle it together until they conquer it. A successful team has a positive outlook and they try to take care of each other. By nurturing the members of your team you will get the best results.

A team that is not successful usually has members that have their own agendas and do work separately. Some members may not pull their part of the load; some may be workaholics, causing resentment among members. If team members are perfectionists, this can cause conflict among members as they cannot meet the high standards and feel they are not successful. Some team leaders do not delegate or share the load. This also causes resentment among members, making those with low self-esteem feel of less value if they do not get to share part of the load.[4]

Pay for help. As our children have gone away to college, we have found that paying for additional help each week has tremendous benefits. With both of us working full time, knowing that the heavy cleaning will be done once a week relieves us of needless pressure. We can spend time during the evening hours enjoying our favorite music, reading books, or talking with each other. We found that by cutting corners on grocery bills, we could pay for this service—a service that has enabled us to have the gift of time and has increased the intimacy in our marriage relationship.

Enjoy the benefits. If you have not been delegating chores to all family members, it will take some time before your home functions smoothly. This transition in family fairness will not be easy, and be prepared for miffed feelings as members, who used to spend evenings playing video games or watching TV, now have to vacuum rugs or clean the kitty litter box. Know that these feelings will pass, especially as the load is divided, and Mom and Dad get to spend extra time together to get to know each other intimately.

Step 3: *Seek support.*

Many married couples depend on support groups within the local church to feel recharged after raising children or caregiving to parents. Curriculum can be studied to enrich family life or the marriage relationship as men and women learn to deal effectively with discipline and time-management problems. Bible studies can help overextended fathers and mothers maintain hope when they feel defeated. And praying with other Christians gives strength to all members as they leave to tackle the awesome responsibility of raising children, caring for aging parents, and increasing intimacy within the marriage.

These relationships with couples in the "same boat as you" are important for many reasons. Not only will you learn how other Christian couples are solving problems at home, you will also have an adult support system during the rough times of raising a family.

Support groups enable you to have a sounding board. You can verbalize your problems without fear of being criticized. Because of the atmosphere of love, caring, and understanding that is cultivated in the friendship, you will be able to ask for guidance when needed.

The minister of your church is an excellent resource for support and guidance in overcoming burnout. If your family problems are too intense, your pastor can recommend professional help. If the situation is temporary, he or she can direct you toward attainable goals that can help during the crucial time.

Step 4: *Self-improvement leads to home-improvement.*

As you work to balance giving to family members with giving to your partner, it is important to maintain your own interests and life, including paying attention to career and personal needs. Yes, fulfilling your needs are important to increase intimacy with your partner.

What are your rights as a person and as a married couple? You have the right to

- *Get angry and express your feelings in an appropriate manner.* Don't forget that you and your partner are the "family managers." Set the home rules, then expect all family members to follow these. If family members don't follow through in their responsibilities, have another family meeting and discuss this openly.
- *Reject attempts by your child or other family members to manipulate you through anger or peer pressure.* Be a "united" front with your mate as you hold firm to rules and protect your marriage relationship from disruption.
- *Receive respect, forgiveness, affection, and acceptance.* These attributes are expected in functional families, and you have the duty to teach your child how to treat you justly.
- *Offer respect, forgiveness, affection, and acceptance.* The best way for children to learn these attributes is for you to model the same.
- *Take pride in your accomplishments and applaud the courage it takes to meet the many demands of life.* If your life is in balance, stand proud!
- *Maintain a full personal life so that when your child grows up and leaves home, you will not be at loose ends.* This is especially important for women. We have seen that when children leave the nest to go on to college or a career, mothers who worked part time or had interests outside the home while raising the children adjusted better than women who focused only on child rearing. Start today to cultivate your

marriage and hobbies so your empty nest days will be fulfilling.

- *Stay involved in the church and attend regularly.* Make spiritual nourishment important not only to your marriage relationship, but also to your family. We all need a source of strength to face life's unexpected interruptions.

- *Seek professional help if you feel overwhelmed.* Call your pastor, doctor, or other professional if you have a concern that is creating havoc in your family. If your children are out of control, talk to another person for help in getting on track with discipline and family time management. If your parents are aging and you are thrust into the caregiving role, seek help from support groups so that problems can be dealt with before they become crisis situations.

- *Know when to draw the line.* The reality is that in order to maintain an intimate relationship with your partner, you sometimes must let go in one area of your life to meet the needs somewhere else. If you are a parent, there may be times when you cannot tuck your child into bed *and* spend an evening out with your partner. If you are a caregiver, there will be times when you may not be able to visit your parent when she needs you because you and your husband have planned some alone time together. Knowing that you will experience these relationship diversions, you can prepare ahead for them and know when to draw the line so that your marriage stays in the forefront.

Week Eight: Don't Let Your Family Fade the Heat

Focus: Today's couples are giving more than ever before with more than fourteen million married couples in which both partners are working outside the home while caring for children and aging parents. To handle the many demands of life while deepening the intimacy in your relationship, you have to learn to take control of your family instead of letting the demands of your family control you. This means that you must love yourself enough to set limits in the family, learn to be "good enough" in all that you do, and delegate home responsibilities so that every member is involved.

Central Bible Truth: "You must love others as much as yourself" (Mark 12:31).

Monday: *Identify the problem.*

Spend today observing your behavior in the family. Do you pick up after children who are old enough to pick up after themselves? Do you stay up late at night organizing the family for the next day—when members could have done this for themselves?

Reflection and response:

Write down all actions you take for family members today, including career, cooking, cleaning, doing dishes, yardwork, helping with homework, and more. Write down the time spent doing each action.

	Action	**Time Spent**
His:	_____	_____
	_____	_____
	_____	_____
Hers:	_____	_____
	_____	_____
	_____	_____

Tuesday: *Learn to draw the line.*

Review your Monday notes and see where your time was spent assisting family members and doing home chores. Was this divided equally among all members? If it wasn't, why not?

Reflection and response:

Talk with your partner about a division of responsibilities in the family. Write down your personal feelings.

His: _____

_____

Hers: _____

_____

Wednesday: *Outline responsibilities.*

Today will be crucial in learning to love yourself more as you outline the specific responsibilities in your home and learn to delegate these fairly among all capable family members.

Reflection and response:

Write down chores using the following categories:

Daily Chores	**Weekly Chores**	**Monthly Chores**
_____	_____	_____
_____	_____	_____
_____	_____	_____

Talk with your partner after making this list and discuss how these responsibilities could be divided fairly, without one person having to shoulder the brunt of home chores. Write down some ideas here:

His: _____

_____

Hers: _____

_____

Thursday: *Set up a family meeting.*

Household responsibilities can be discussed and delegated at a family meeting with all members present. Allow each person a chance to offer suggestions or voice complaints, but, ultimately, you and your partner preside as you outline the needs of the family and fill in who will take care of what. At the family meeting you will need to let the members know what each job entails and negotiate differences in opinions.

Reflection and response:

Using the list you made on Wednesday, put names next to the specific responsibilities. Post this list in your kitchen (the refrigerator is a great place!) as a reminder to members to get their tasks completed. Don't forget that you and your partner are the "family managers." If the responsibilities are not done by members, then follow through appropriately with the consequences.

Friday: *Hear the wake-up call.*

Are you being "good enough" or do you overdo it with giving to everyone except yourself and your spouse?

Reflection and response:

Talk openly about how you perceive your partner and his or her relationships with other family members. Do you think your partner tries too hard to fill everyone's needs and ignores her own? Perhaps you see your partner as too busy parenting or caregiving to give attention to you. Use the following checklist to measure your partner's response to living on a fast track:

His   **Hers**

_____   _____ Family members complain that you are grouchy.

_____   _____ The noise-level and busyness of the home bother you.

_____   _____ The children seem out of control to you.

_____   _____ You spend a great deal of time yelling at family members.

_____   _____ The children do not listen to you.

_____   _____ You have become forgetful and stumble with words.

_____   _____ There is more conflict between the children.

Write down your thoughts along with a suggestion that may help your partner learn to break the habit of being all things to all people.

His: _____

_____

Hers: _____

_____

Saturday: *Learn to say no.*

As you learn to stop family members from blocking any chance you might have of an intimate marriage, it is important to learn to say no to demands that are not urgent. Part of being able to really say no depends on how you feel about yourself.

Assertiveness psychology, an approach to building and maintaining self-respect, says the more you stand up for yourself and act in a manner you respect, the more you will be comfortable with yourself. By exercising basic rights of being a person, you can change your attitudes and feelings about yourself.[5] And, choosing your involvement in life is your basic right as a child of God. In other words, it is okay to say no sometimes and mean it!

Reflection and response:

Saying no is just the opposite of saying yes. And it takes practice. Write down some areas where you need to be assertive and say no to unimportant demands family members place on you—especially if they are capable of taking care of these demands themselves.

His: _____

_____

Hers: _____

_____

Sunday: *Set priorities.*

Talk with your partner today about the many family demands that you have, whether raising children or caregiving. In the midst of your responsibilities to loved ones, your foremost responsibility should be to each other. Studies have shown that when couples sacrifice their relationship to meet the needs of children, there is a greater feeling of loneliness and emptiness. It does not have to be this way.

Reflection and response:

Set some personal, marital, and family goals for today, including some quality time with your partner, your children or parents, and yourself. Putting these goals on paper will enable you to realize them—for they can only become a reality as you stop busying yourself with less important matters. Household chores are never done, so we have to put them in perspective. Spending time with those we love requires a plan, and we have to initiate the action or we will never take the time that is so necessary.

What are your goals for not letting the family fade the heat?

His: _____

_____

Hers: _____

_____

9

Face Life's Interruptions ... Together

"We finally got the mortgage paid off on the house and were looking forward to retirement, when our son was diagnosed with cancer. After a lengthy course of treatment, they finally gave him one year to live. We felt as if our lives were over."

—Elizabeth, age 53

"Our last child left for college, and for the first time in our lives we felt a relief from responsibility; then Sharon's dad was diagnosed with Alzheimer's disease. He has been living with us ever since."

—Raymond, age 45

"We'd only been married for six years when Pete's company went out of business. He lost his job, and we lost our new home. Why did this happen to us?"

—Stephanie, age 29

"We are both so healthy and life was good, but when our first child was four years old, he was diagnosed with leukemia. I feel like our lives will never be the same."

—Kelly, age 24

"We've worked hard all our lives, then after our son's car accident, we were sued and lost everything we had. There's nothing to live for anymore."

—Kevin, age 48

"Our life was perfect. Daniel was just asked to be a partner in a prestigious law practice when he was diagnosed with cancer. How could something so horrible happen to someone so strong and young? What did we do wrong?"

—Michelle, age 33

What Kind of God Is This?

Perhaps you are wondering exactly what kind of God would let suffering occur to Christians who are "on the same team." One fine Christian woman we know has suffered for two decades with multiple sclerosis (MS), a chronic disease that gradually weakens and paralyzes the body. She has been amazed at some of the advice she has received from friends and relatives.

A few typical examples include,

"You must really like to be sick; you bring so much of it on yourself." That comment was from a nearby relative who never even sent a get-well card.

Another relative confided, "The reason I have perfect health is because I think right. Nobody gets sick if they are doing the 'right' things in life."

Her best friend quipped, "I know what it is like to be crippled. I had a really bad case of tennis elbow last year that put me out of commission."

Then a member of her Sunday school class added, "God must cherish you to trust you with this burden."

Perhaps the last comment was the most startling as her pastor seriously said, "I know you fake your limp to try to get attention."

What kind of God do some people have? Perhaps we can learn from the time when Jesus and his disciples passed a man who was blind at birth. "Who sinned," asked Jesus' disciples, "this man or his parents, that he was born blind?"

What kind of God did these disciples have? Did they think that God looks down from a throne in heaven and says, "All right, fellow. I know that you've been cheating on your taxes and hitting your wife, so I'm going to take that precious baby in your wife's womb and strike it blind to teach you a lesson. That'll show you."

Sound far-fetched? You probably know of a friend or loved one who has experienced a similar tragedy. Perhaps you have personally lived with tragedy in your own life and have carried around a burden of guilt. Deep down you have a feeling that God is punishing you for something you have done by hurting someone you love very much. We ask again, What kind of God is that?

Pain seems to go hand in hand with life's interruptions. Eugene C. Kennedy describes the worst feeling about pain: "It does not kill us; we never die of pain, although we sometimes wish we could, if only to put an end to it. And the worst pains are those which seem to have no remedies, the ones that tear the edges of our spirit because they come when we are healthy rather than when we are sick. We may try to tranquilize these pains away, but eventually the ache returns. They even go on vacation with us, waiting for an idle moment, or a favorite song to use as an entrance into our hearts. What is this pain that will not kill us, this ache that has learned how to follow us so closely through life?"[1]

Exploration:

- Have you felt the "pain" of life's interruptions personally? In your marriage? Did you feel that God was punishing you?
- Name some recent pains you have felt. How did these affect your emotions? Your spiritual life? Your marriage relationship?

Charting Your Intimate Journey

By now you have completed the Intimate Journey outlined in this book. It is important to understand that all the pages you read and actions you took were not in vain. We wrote these to enable you and your partner to experience an emotional closeness far greater than you ever have before. Why? So that when life's interruptions hit, you will have an inner strength with which to cope and a strong hand to guide you through the storm.

You see, each of us will have to face tragedy at some point in our life, some more than others; some sooner than others. But the greatest asset we can have, aside from the strength and power of Christ Jesus as our personal Savior, is abiding love and support from our spiritual soul mate—our partner in marriage. And this can only happen if we are truly one in body, mind, and spirit, if we have taken time to nurture intimacy in our relationship.

But What *If* the Worst Happens?

Have you ever wondered what you and your partner would do if "the worst happens"? What would be the "worst" for you—the loss of a child, a terminal illness, loss of your job? Every minute of every day people face life's worst possibilities—a child who is fatally injured in a car accident or who drowns in the neighbor's swimming pool; a parent who is diagnosed with a terminal illness just before retirement age or who falls victim to a heinous crime; a company that goes bankrupt leaving employees without income and families without health insurance. Yes, the worst can and does happen every day.

But what good will our love for each other be *if and when* the very worst happens in our lives? This is an intensely personal question. Ask yourselves, *What will we do as a couple, as a team, if the worst should happen?* For many, this question will breed an anxiety and fear that runs deeper than your optimism, your faith, and even your love for each other.

When the very worst seems imminent, it is quite often enough to divide a marriage. Jacques and Alice were married ten years when Alice got pregnant for the first time. They said they were ecstatic, as they had tried for years to conceive and had even had fertility treatments, but to no avail until now. Now they were having a baby. Early sonogram tests showed that the baby was a boy, Jacques' namesake, and nothing could stop his enthusiasm. Then Alice's doctor's appointment at eight months put a halt on their entire life's plan. The doctor told the couple that he could no longer hear a heartbeat from the baby. More tests, another sonogram, then another consultation with the doctor confirmed what they feared most: The baby was dead, and labor had to be induced immediately.

Alice grieved openly, telling us that this was a "nightmare" in her life, having to live with her dead son's body inside her womb for thirty-six painful hours. Jacques held all his emotions inside, never once letting on that he was in grief.

After the delivery and the funeral, Jacques left Alice. She later told us that there was no fight, no argument; he said that he didn't ever want to grieve like that again. Life's unplanned interruption also interrupted their marriage.

After talking further with Alice we realized that she and

Jacques had had a strained relationship for years. "Intimately bonded?" she questioned. "I never felt as if Jacques really knew me."

But in order to have enough strength to get through a crisis, such as Alice and Jacques experienced, it is vital to know each other and to be intimately bonded with a marriage centered in Christ Jesus. We all must begin by realizing that "the very worst" is not a stranger to those who have set out to follow our Lord. We have *no* guarantees that we will be insulated from the worst life has to offer. However, it has been our conviction that the best in life is always more powerful than the worst. And the best can be experienced right now as you make intimate decisions that bring you closer together and closer to the cross.

The old prophets and disciples who nourished our faith were not protected from the worst in life. But when the worst came upon them, they sought God's lessons in it. With discernment and vision, they traced the results of man's inhumanity and pointed the way back to God.

Our faith was born in a stable and confirmed on a cross. The Church was still an infant when Stephen was martyred and the disciples scattered. It seemed like the worst had happened. But out of what seemed to be the very worst arose Paul, a new man who could bring the gospel to a waiting world. It looked like the worst had happened when Rome with its stability of government was destroyed, but the advance of Attila the Hun opened the way for a mighty march of faith. It looked like the worst had happened when Martin Luther was excommunicated from the church he loved. But that didn't stop him.

Perhaps the very worst will sweep over your family someday. When this happens, what will you do?

Exploration:

- Name your greatest fear.
- What would the "worst" be in your lives right now?
- If the "worst" happened right now, how would you cope?
- How have other married friends or family members coped when life's storms came crashing down?

Continue to Be Our Best

When the worst happens, we must continue to be our very best. Because when we experience the very worst in the storms of life and continue to be our very best, the kingdom of God surges forward. God blesses our persistence and faithfulness.

The Bible tells us of Nehemiah, who against all odds and in the face of threats within and without, built the wall of Jerusalem as he leaned on faith in God. The Bible also tells us of Gideon, who had only three hundred men to face the armed might of the enemy. While it seemed absurd for him to stay and fight, with faith in God, he won. George Washington should have surrendered many times. Even his own countrymen were indifferent to the cause, and his trusted generals betrayed him. But neither treachery, injustice, cold, hunger, or the sight of the enemy could shake his resolve. With his strong faith in God, a new nation was born.

A story is reported of a frail African-American girl who was paralyzed. Her mother was told by many that this child would never walk again. The mother and the girl refused to stop trying. Together, painfully, they worked until she could stumble, and then walk, and then finally run. In 1961, Wilma Rudolph won more Olympic medals than any woman track star in history.

What if the worst happens? Well, the worst has happened to billions of people before us. But those who rise above life's interruptions, clinging to their faith in God and to each other, are able to accomplish great things . . . even in the worst of times. Life's interruptions can plant the sign of the cross upon us so that when we stand before God, he will know that we belong to him. Those who have stood before the very worst the world can offer are marked with the sign of our faith . . . the cross.

As he lay dying, the great artist Michelangelo said, "God did not create me to abandon me." And he never will. What about in your relationship? If you have nurtured an intimate relationship before life's interruptions occur, when the worst happens, God's love and your abiding love for each other will remain.

Exploration:

- Which best describes your marital relationship before reading this book and taking the daily actions? Which describes it now?
    a. needs renewal
    b. renewal in progress
    c. renewal halted
- Recall a time when your marriage was at an all-time low because of life's interruptions. Describe this. How have you moved beyond that? What did you learn from the moment? How would you react differently now?
- In what ways has the Christian hope of eternal life given you hope during life's interruptions?

Two Sources of Sufferings

As you consider the question "what if the worst happens," it is important to understand the suffering you will face as life's interruptions surface. There are two sources of suffering in this world, and we can experience one or both, depending on the choices we make.

One source is sin. When we break God's laws or nature's laws, we sin and we suffer. That is built into the very fabric of life. If you walk out into the middle of the street and step in front of a speeding car, do you lie there and ask, "Oh, dear Lord. Why did this happen to me?" Of course not! You know why it happened. You broke the law. When we break laws, we pay. Most of the unfortunate suffering in our lives takes place because we break God's laws.

The other source of suffering is the natural order. Do you really believe that God sent Hurricane Hugo to devastate the coastal areas of South Carolina to punish those people for their sins? Do you believe that the devastation of the San Francisco earthquake was God's judgment on the people of the Bay area? If so, then why didn't these disasters destroy the casinos in Atlantic City and Las Vegas? Or the crack houses in New York? Or the porno stores in San Francisco? For that matter, why didn't they destroy your home or ours, for we are also sinners.

There are, of course, other explanations of suffering we can consider. We live in the most majestic world imaginable, but it is a world where there are hurricanes, earthquakes, floods, viruses, and defective genes. None of these are sent by God to punish us. Jesus said, "He makes his sun rise on the evil and on the good, and sends rain on the just and on the unjust" (Matthew 5:45, RSV). The natural order contains both good and evil. The writer of Genesis claims that it was because of Adam's sin that this happened. Man not only became alienated from God after Adam sinned but even from the very earth, which is his home. This is one explanation. Another is that this world is but a laboratory, a preparatory school, if you will. God is in the business of creating souls fit to dwell with him in eternity. So he has given us obstacles to overcome. Why? That is the only way we grow.

When our youngest child was born, she was diagnosed with a congenital eye problem, esotropia or crossed eyes. We were devastated. We were both healthy, and our other two children had very straight eyes. What did we do wrong?

Assured by several pediatric ophthalmologists that we "did nothing wrong"—these things just happen—we felt some comfort. Ashley had surgery to correct the problem, and after years of therapy and doctor's appointments, she now has straight eyes.

Although you could not have told us at the time, we experienced later that this was just one of life's many interruptions, and we grew into a deeper understanding of life and love through this as we leaned on each other and Christ Jesus through the surgery and treatment.

Benjamin and Carla's only son was born with a rare blood disorder, and although he lived for five years, he was in and out of hospitals the entire time. "There was no treatment for Kenny," Carla shared. "We had tried to have a family for eleven years when Kenny was born, so we knew this was God's miracle. When the doctor's told us he wouldn't live to be a year old, we were devastated. How could God do this to us? Why didn't he choose another family who already had children? We went to church each week and were good people. Why us?

"I think that Kenny taught us how to be accepting and to love each other during the five years we had him," she continued. "We came to realize that God had given us a most special gift with Kenny. He was always brave, intuitive, and courageous, even when he had to wear an IV around while playing. Through loving Kenny and caring for him, we learned how to care for each other and to love God. Oh, yes, we miss our son, but we have no anger or regrets. We are better people, we are God's people, for having gone through this experience."

Exploration:

As Christians, God calls us to grow in faith. As a married couple, what areas do you need to grow in?
- faith
- love for each other
- trust in God
- patience
- acceptance
- hope

We Are *Not* in Control

If only we were masters of our destinies! So many of us feel that if we only work hard enough, we will be successful and not have trials in life. We feel that if only we are obedient to God and to each other, then tragedy will not come our way. Life doesn't work this way. Although diligence and obedience are necessary for living a godly life, there are things that are out of our control.

But don't most of us feel helpless when we hear that we have no control? That is where faith comes in, and faith is the conviction that there is One who is in control, whose nature is love.

Sometimes that is a faint hope to hold on to. Fatigue and desperation tell us, "Throw in the towel; give up." How often we need to remember the words of the psalmist: "Take delight in the Lord, and he will give you the desires of your heart. Commit your way to the Lord; trust in him, and he will act" (Psalm 37:4–5, RSV).

By yielding control of our lives and trusting God, waiting can be a creative strategy for dealing with life's interruptions.

A beautiful story is told of an elderly woman who sold flowers in a busy downtown area. It was the day after Easter, and the pastor of the downtown church paused for a moment at the top of the steps leading from his church to the avenue. Everyone was busy rushing to their jobs, yet this woman sat on the ground with corsages and boutonnieres spread out in front of her.

The flower lady was smiling, her wrinkled face alive with joy. The pastor started down the stairs, then on an impulse turned and picked up a flower.

As he put it in his lapel, he said, "You look so happy this morning."

"Why not?" she replied. "Everything is so good."

She was so shabbily dressed and seemed so very old that her reply startled this man. "No troubles at all?" he responded.

"Pastor, you cannot reach my age and not have troubles," she replied. "Only it's like Jesus and Good Friday." The elderly woman paused for a moment.

"Yes?" prompted the pastor.

"Well, when Jesus was crucified on Good Friday, that was the worst day for the whole world. And when I get troubles, I remember that. And then I think what happened only three days later—Easter and our Lord arising. So when I get troubles, I have learned to wait three days—somehow everything seems to look better and get all right again."

And she smiled goodbye.

The elderly flower lady's advice would help many of us: "Give God a chance to help; wait three days."

Think about it. In the midst of life's interruptions when we have lost all control of what is happening to ourselves or our loved ones, what else can we do but *wait, watch,* and *work*? Such waiting requires humility and faith simply to persevere. Sometimes, however, waiting can be a strategic response to a difficult situation.

There are areas of our life beyond our control and for good reason. We simply cannot ever hope to have enough knowledge or enough wisdom to perfectly determine our lives. As someone has wisely said, "If God would concede me his omnipotence for twenty-four hours, you would see how many changes I would make in the world. But if he gave me his wisdom, too, I would leave things just as they are."

Thomas Carlyle once wrote, "Does the minnow understand the ocean tides and periodic currents, the trade winds and the monsoons and the moon's eclipses, by all of which the condition of its little creek is regulated, and may, from time to time, be quite overset and reversed? Such a minnow is man; his creek, this planet earth; his ocean, the immeasurable all; his monsoons and periodic currents, the mysterious course of providence."

This is where the Christian relies not on luck or upon superstition, but upon faith in a wise and loving God. Paul writes those familiar words in Romans 8:28: "We know that in everything God works for good with those who love him, who are called according to his purpose" (RSV). That is the essence of the gospel. It does not fit our rationalistic view of the universe. It makes a mockery of our dependence upon charms and astrologers, but it is the gospel. In everything, God is working for good with those who love him.

Life's Interruptions Have No Quick Fix

Recently we were taping a nature show on television and made an error in editing out the commercials. Our intent was to tape the show and remove all commercials with the pause button on the remote control. However, we somehow got out of sync and ended up taping only the commercials and editing out the show.

This mistake is not terribly different from what many of us end up doing with real life. We want a quick fix—something to make all of life's moments string together as fun and excitement without any interruptions. Then we discover that quick fixes just do not work. Life simply is not designed so we can edit out all the trials, hardships, and crises. We learn, we grow, we mature as we deal with life's many hardships.

Just as there are but two sources of suffering—sin and the natural order—there is only one source of healing for relationships facing life's interruptions. That source is God. When Jesus answered his disciples about the blind man, he said, "It was not that this man who sinned, or his parents, but that the works of God might be made manifest in him" (John 9:3, RSV). All healing comes from God. He is a God of health and wholeness; in fact, healing is God's will for our lives—whether our need is spiritual, emotional, or physical. God wants us well.

Think about it. God has planted healing in the very world he has created. A generation ago, there were diseases ravaging this planet that we don't even think of anymore. As the growth of medical technology and knowledge continues to accelerate, there will be even more progress in the generations to come. We don't create cures, but we do discover what God has already ordained.

We were reading recently about a medical team that is working in the Amazon jungle under a five-year contract with the National Cancer Institute to find the next generation of anticancer drugs. Scientists report finding a certain flower that can reduce white blood cell counts, actually bringing about remissions in leukemia cases. While we know that penicillin comes from a mold, did you know that cortisone is derived from yams? Atropine, a drug for stomach ulcers, comes from belladonna plants. Nutritionists are now reporting incredible healing benefits that can be derived from eating vitamins, minerals, antioxidants, and phytochemicals—all found in natural food products. The world is filled with God's healing properties, if we trust him and believe that he will unleash these.

But Why?

However, when life's interruptions occur, we become far removed from thoughts of God's healing. Instead, we want answers and explanations, and we want them now. As Christians, we must know that there is no way to explain life's interruptions, and it should not be an explanation that we seek. What we should seek is the ability to absorb the tragedy and to respond to the God who has not promised explanations, but who instead provides the grace we need to endure. At such a time, we don't need answers, but we do need strength and hope, and the Scriptures teach us that God will not leave us comfortless. Just as we teach our children that decisions about their sexual morals or alcohol habits cannot be made in the backseat of a car, we must also know that decisions regarding faith and inner strength must be made in calmer, reflective moments.

So it is as we grow in years of marriage, we must not wait until we face life's interruptions to decide to become emotionally bonded with our partner. We need to be taking steps now to face what life has to offer together—with actions to strengthen our marriage and our faith.

Now this inner strength is not a quiet acceptance of "fate." Job didn't stifle his protests, nor did the psalmists, neither did Jesus in the garden or in his cries from the cross. What really matters, however, is not our protests, but how we come through the crisis in the end. And how we will come through life's interruptions will be determined by decisions we make right now. What our faith in God and love for each other do later depend on decisions we make today.

We believe in Christ binding our marriage together, not because he gives us the best "explanation" of human suffering, but because he gives us the strength we both need to live together in harmony and intimacy, and bond together in love so that we become *one—the Bruce team*—against what life has to offer.

Lean on Your Savior, Christ Jesus

Think about it. The name Jesus does not mean "Explainer," but "Savior." And when a loved one dies suddenly, your partner becomes seriously ill, or you suffer from loss of income, a savior is what you will need. The story of Christ's suffering, the way in which he was hounded to his death, says more to us than any argument about why suffering is allowed in God's universe. For if innocent suffering is what horrifies, then here in Christ Jesus is the greatest imaginable suffering and the greatest innocence.

The God we both know and love knows all about suffering. He knows what we feel when our child has surgery. He knows how we hurt when our parents suffer or become ill. He knows what it is like to struggle to try to make ends meet or to lose a job or to get demoted in our career. He knows what it is like to lose a best friend or to live with a friend's anger. And he knows what it is like to stand beside a loved one's grave. You see, he has been there; there is no interruption that God has not known and from which he cannot rescue us.

Look at the Options

As we get in touch with the reality of interruptions, we need to become in tune with the choices we have in life. *If* we choose to remain distant to our partners and to God, what options do we have when tragedy hits? One option is to *stay with the protest and let a mood of anger and bitterness sour our lives.* You've seen people who have done this.

Another possibility is what we consider a *stoic* one. There are people who simply shrug their shoulders and resign themselves to the grim road ahead. For some strange reason, don't most of us tend to admire these people? But we are dissatisfied with that response because this approach causes the spirit within to die. The stoic settles for fatalism rather than for a God of love, mercy, and grace. The stoic tends to lose sensitivity to the other's sorrow, expecting the same tight-lipped approach to life's problems from all. Believe us when we say that Christ Jesus was no stoic.

There is a third and better way. Notice that we call this a "way" and not an "explanation." Arguments and explanations fall silent when we are in darkness, when life's interruptions hit, but we have experienced that there is always a light, a way, if you will. When we join hands together in an intimate marriage and look at this light, we realize that *we are not alone*. This light is what we call the "communion of saints." We know that in the midst of tragedy or crisis, we are surrounded by men and women, a "cloud of witnesses," who went through suffering, trusting boldly in God. They aren't here to offer us explanations, but they have given us the testimony of their lives to point us to a Savior who can see us through to victory.

The apostle Paul was the victim of as much unjust suffering and tragedy as any human being except our Lord. Yet still he wrote, "I consider that the sufferings of this present time are not worth comparing with the glory that is to be revealed to us . . . because the creation itself will be set free from its bondage to decay and obtain the glorious liberty of the children of God" (Romans 8:18, 21, RSV).

Paul urges us later in that same chapter to yield to the Spirit who helps us in our weakness, for we don't know how to pray, and we must depend on the Spirit of Christ to intercede on our behalf with sighs too deep even for words.

Exploration:

- Seriously consider, if you knew that you only had five days to live, what would you do?
- What if your partner only had five days to live? How would you relate? What would you say? Would you have any regrets?

Get Me to the Promised Land

Perhaps the real problem we face in our marriages and in life is that we all want to get to the promised land without going through the wilderness. You've heard people say, "I want it all!" While that may seem ideal, life doesn't work that way.

There is a popular phrase that "life is a jungle"—and it is. Just as in a jungle we will trip over branches, get bitten by poisonous snakes, be forced to climb the tallest trees—sometimes even fall out of them—and feel very alone and afraid. We don't know about you but if we had to walk through a jungle right now, we would make sure that we were together—side by side—*the Bruce team*—bonded in Christ Jesus.

The same is true with life. No matter who you are or how much money you have or how well educated you are, you are going to face life's interruptions at some time. Most of these interruptions will come through loss, death, failing health, financial setback, or broken friendships. No life on earth is ever free of such emotionally painful experiences, and there is no way to avoid them. They are part of the reality of existence.[2] But wouldn't it be better to face them together, intimately bonded in a Christ-centered marriage, than all alone?

Over the past twenty-three years, our marriage has changed and has been redefined by the interruptions we've had to face, such as having a child with a chronic illness, hospitalizations and medical bills, job stresses, moving, close friends diagnosed with terminal illnesses, untimely and sudden deaths of personal friends and family members, the suicide of our child's close friend at age twelve, raising three independent teens, and more. But because we stood strong as *the Bruce team* against these experiences, we have enjoyed growth and deeper intimacy. In time our pain has subsided, and we have discovered that the most valuable thing we possess is an untiring love for each other and for God through Christ Jesus.

Realize That God Knows Your Feelings

No matter how difficult your life is or becomes, it is important to know that God is there; he feels our pain and sorrow. The Scripture in the Psalms affirms his grief: "You have seen me tossing and turning through the night. You have collected all my tears and preserved them in your bottle! You have recorded every one in your book" (Psalm 56:8). But God also sees when we act in ways that honor him, when we uphold Christlike standards of living. Zephaniah 3:17 celebrates this rejoicing, saying, " 'He will rejoice over you in great gladness; he will love you and not accuse you.' Is that a joyous choir I hear? No, it is the Lord himself exulting over you in happy song."

While we don't always know why God places us where he does in life, we do know that as difficult as our life situations may be, he is with us and has a plan for us.

Continue to Use Your Journal

As you face life's interruptions in days to come, continue to journal as you record the events in your lives each day. This will take some soul-searching as you evaluate uncomfortable situations, identify their feelings, name spiritual experiences, and get in touch with how you personally act and react when confronted with life's interruptions. This writing each day will also enable you to gradually eliminate less desirable thoughts you may have about situations, such as loneliness, depression, and anger, then begin to build a deeper awareness, focusing on understanding God's will for your life.

Lean on His Word for Strength

The apostle Paul reminds us in Romans 12 and 1 Timothy 4 to practice the skills the Bible teaches. This is crucial for all of us as we try to nurture an intimate journey with our partner in the midst of life's interruptions. We work out physically by climbing stairs, swimming, doing aerobics, and more to get in touch with our body and to develop it. The same is true with spiritual disciplines, such as Bible study, prayer, worship, and fellowship with other Christians. We do this to embrace our spiritual side and to develop our relationship with God.

As discussed in Week One, acknowledging one's faith in Jesus as Lord and Savior is the beginning of a personal relationship, a faith walk, with him. Then spiritual growth takes time just like physical growth; it takes time for God to work in the life of the believer and create a new being.

See Each Day As an Opportunity to Share God's Love

Christ's love is other-centered, no matter where we are. Once we have yielded to the love of Christ, this is the way we act—naturally reaching out to others. A former criminal, Kozlov, later a church leader, writes of life in a Soviet prison:

> Among the general despair, while prisoners like myself were cursing ourselves, the camp, the authorities; while we opened up our veins, or our stomachs, or hanged ourselves; the Christians (often with sentences of twenty to twenty-five years) did not despair. One could see Christ reflected in their faces. Their pure, upright life, deep faith and devotion to God, their gentleness and their wonderful manliness, became a shining example of real life for thousands.[3]

This is authentic Christianity, whenever and wherever it appears. As Christ-centered people, faith is not to be lived out just at church or before close friends; Christians are called to share God's grace with all people. Read Matthew 5:15–16: "Don't hide your light! Let it shine for all; let your good deeds glow for all to see, so that they will praise your heavenly Father."

Even though you and your spouse may be undergoing trials and tribulations, continue to let others know that you are Christians through such behaviors as generosity, gentleness, patience, a smile and kindness, among many. These attributes will show that you are following God's way—even though you may be facing life's interruptions.

The choice is before us all. We can choose to stand alone each day and face the trials, tragedies, or change that comes without the support of our partner. If we do, our marriage will surely stagnate and our union will be weakened. Or we can choose to work daily on the intimate bond in our marriage, then welcome the opportunity for growth and change as we face life's challenges.

And the Greatest of These Is Hope

Has the intimacy dwindled in your marriage? Have you and your spouse lost the very commitment you need to support each other in this sacred Christian relationship so that when life's interruptions come, you can cope with these as a team? Remember the promise of the Scripture found in Job 14:7: "For there is hope for a tree—if it's cut down it sprouts again, and grows tender, new branches."

The choice is ours to make, but we know that even in the worst relationships, there is hope. Many Christians agree with the statement, "the greatest of these is hope." Norman Cousins has said that "the capacity for hope is the most significant fact of life. It provides human beings with a sense of destination and the energy to get started."[4]

When life's interruptions occur, most of us temporarily misplace our faith and go back to acting as if we had never heard the gospel. We do this even though we know that faith is our greatest ally. It is important to know that those who trust in a good and just God never lose hope. They are perennial optimists. Such faith is of great benefit in dealing with some of our greatest fears.

Cancer researchers at King's College Hospital in London did a long-term study of fifty-seven breast-cancer victims who had undergone mastectomies. They found that seven out of ten women "with a fighting spirit" were alive ten years later, while four out of five women "who felt hopeless" at the diagnosis had died.

Henry Ward Beecher once said, "Every day has two handles; we can take hold of it with the handle of anxiety or with the handle of faith."

There is something about the presence of the Master in our lives and in our marriage that gives us a sense of calm, even in the presence of life's interruptions. Only Christ Jesus can calm the storms as he speaks: "Take heart, it is I; have no fear"(Matthew 14:27, RSV).

There is great hope for marriages today. In this great Age of Anxiety, when it seems more tempting to block intimacy from our lives and huddle behind closed doors, there is One who can penetrate those doors, who shows us his hands and his sides and who says to us, "Peace be with you." That hope is found in the person of Christ Jesus for he alone has the authority and the power to heal all who ask. Trust in him today as you reclaim intimacy in your marriage.

Notes

Introduction

1. Lawrence A. Sagan, *The Health of Nations* (New York: Basic Books, Inc., 1987).
2. Lori H. Gordon, Ph.D., "Intimacy: The Art of Working Out Your Relationships," *Psychology Today* (September/October 1992), pp. 43, 80.
3. Mark Clements, "Sex in America Today," *Parade Magazine* (August 7, 1994), pp. 4–5.

Chapter One

1. *Life and Work Pursuits: Bible Studies for Adults* (Nashville: The Sunday School Board, July 23, 1995), p. 35.
2. Dr. M. Scott Peck, "How to Know Yourself Much, Much Better," *BottomLife Personal* (Greenwich, Conn.: Boardroom, Inc., April 1994), p. 1.
3. Ellie Kahn, "Feeling Good About Yourself," *Parents* magazine (May 1990), p. 98.
4. Maxie Dunnam, *The Workbook on Spiritual Disciplines* (Nashville: The Upper Room, 1984), p. 15.
5. *The Spirit-Filled Christian* (Colorado Springs: NavPress, 1984), p. 14.
6. Harold Koenig and Andrew J. Weaver, "Faith Eases Potential

Aches and Pains of Aging," *The United Methodist Reporter* (July 29, 1994), p. 4.

7. Victor M. Parachin, "Eight Ways to Grow Spiritually," *Key to Christian Education* (Spring 1994), p. 6.

8. Georgianna Summers, *Teaching As Jesus Taught* (Nashville: Discipleship Resources, 1983), p. 49.

9. Muriel James, *Born to Win* (New York: Addison-Wesley, 1976), p. 36.

10. Leo Buscaglia, Ph.D., *Personhood* (New York: Fawcett, 1984), p. 87.

Chapter Two

1. Leo Buscaglia, Ph.D., *Bus Nine to Paradise* (Thorofare, N.J.: SLACK, Inc., 1986), p. 27.

2. Dr. M. Scott Peck, "Men and Women: The Secrets of Getting Along Much, Much Better," *BottomLine Personal* (Greenwich, Conn.: Boardroom, Inc., February 1995), p. 1.

3. Ari Kiev, M.D., *How to Keep Love Alive* (New York: Harper and Row, 1982), p. 76.

4. Harriet Goldhor Lerner, Ph.D., *The Dance of Intimacy* (New York: Harper and Row, 1989), p. 3.

5. Muriel James, *Born to Win* (New York: Addison-Wesley, 1976), p. 108.

6. Leo Buscaglia, Ph.D., *Living, Loving, and Learning* (New York: Fawcett, 1985), p. 84.

7. Buscaglia, *Born for Love* (New York: Random House, 1992), p. 166.

8. Debra Fulghum Bruce, *Making Memories That Count* (Springfield, Mo.: Chrism, 1994), pp. 66–69.

9. New York: HarperCollins, 1992.

10. Peck, "Men and Women: The Secrets of Getting Along Much, Much Better," p. 1.

11. Theodore Isaac Rubin, M.D., *The Angry Book* (New York: Macmillan, 1969), p. 174.

12. *Life and Work Pursuits: Adult Bible Studies* (Nashville: The Sunday School Board, November 5, 1995), p. 53.

13. Ari Kiev, M.D., *How to Keep Love Alive*, p. 76.

14. Lee Salk, M.D., *Familyhood* (New York: Simon and Schuster, 1992), p. 31.

Chapter Three

1. Leo Buscaglia, Ph.D., *Loving Each Other* (Thorofare, N.J.: SLACK, Inc., 1984), p. 54.
2. Pam McKeown, "Get Over It—Overcoming the Psychology of Victimization," *The University of Oklahoma Health Sciences Center* (1995), p. 1.
3. Harvill Hendrix, Ph.D., "Ten Ways to Get What You Want," *Family Circle* (April 1992), p. 31.
4. Buscaglia, *Bus Nine to Paradise* (Thorofare, N.J.: SLACK, Inc., 1986), p. 225.
5. Dr. Barry Lubetkin, "How to Let Go of a Grudge," *BottomLine Personal* (Greenwich, Conn.: Boardroom, Inc., May 15, 1994), p. 1.
6. "Dr. Diane Ackerman's Secrets of a Much, Much Better Relationship," *BottomLine Personal* (March 1, 1995), p. 9.
7. "Discover It! Conflict Resolution," *Christian Education Counselor* (January 1994), p. 4.
8. Redford Williams, M.D., "Your Anger Can Kill You: How to Control It," *Health Confidential* (April 1994), p. 5.
9. "Cease-Fire," *First* (October 24, 1994), p. 24.
10. Buscaglia, *Born for Love* (New York: Random House, 1992), p. 99.
11. Baylor College of Medicine pamphlet on communications, p. 3.
12. Buscaglia, *Loving Each Other*, p. 54.
13. Harriet Goldhor Lerner, Ph.D., *The Dance of Intimacy* (New York: Harper and Row, 1989), p. 3.
14. Judith Sills, Ph.D., "How to Deal with Anger," *Family Circle* (October 11, 1994), p. 93.
15. Buscaglia, *Born for Love*, p. 89.

Chapter Four

1. William H. Masters, et al., *Masters and Johnson on Sex and Human Loving* (Boston, Toronto: Little, Brown & Company, 1985), p. 304.
2. Barbara de Angelis, *How to Make Love All the Time* (New York: Dell, 1987), p. 144.
3. Allan Decker, M.S.W., L.C.S.W., "Intimacy in Marriage: Role

Mates or Soul Mates?" *Living Well Today* (September/October 1995), p. 1.

4. Warren Farrell, *The Myth of Male Power* (New York: Simon & Schuster, 1993).

5. Marjorie Hansen Shaevitz, *Super Woman Syndrome* (New York: Warner Books, 1984), p. 57.

6. John Gray, Ph.D., "Secrets of Rekindling Romance and Passion," *BottomLine Personal* (Greenwich, Conn.: Boardroom, Inc., August 1995), p. 9.

7. Annie Mayer, *How to Stay Lovers* (Los Angeles: Price, Stern, Sloan, 1990), p. 75.

8. Leo Buscaglia, Ph.D., *Living, Loving, and Learning* (New York: Fawcett, 1992), p. 237.

9. Buscaglia, *Loving Each Other* (Thorofare, N.J.: SLACK, Inc., 1984), p. 137.

10. Decker, loc. cit.

11. Judith Sills, Ph.D., "How to Get the Love You Need," *Family Circle* (April 1995), p. 32.

12. De Angelis, op. cit., p. 143.

Chapter Five

1. Roger B. Szuch, L.C.S.W., "All Work and No Play . . . Is Your Life Out of Balance?" *Living Well Today.* (1992), p. 1.

2. "Work Ethic" quote by Fran Tarkenton, *Better Families*, Vol. 17, No. 11 (November 1993), p. 2.

3. Szuch, loc. cit.

Chapter Six

1. Quoted with permission: Rev. Bill Scott, Jacksonville, Florida (September 1995).

2. *Health* (October 1994), p. 46.

3. Ronald G. Nathan, Thomas E. Staats, and Paul J. Rosch, *The Doctor's Guide to Instant Stress Relief* (New York: G. P. Putnam's Sons, 1987), p. 39.

4. Brent Q. Hafen, *The Health Effects of Attitudes, Emotions, Relationships* (Ashland, Ohio: EMS Associates, 1992), p. 255.

5. Maxie Dunnam, *The Workbook on Coping as Christians* (Nashville: Upper Room, 1988), p. 63.

6. Judith Viorst, *Redbook* (October 1994), p. 14.
7. Herbert Benson, M.D., *The Wellness Book* (New York: Carol Publishing Group, 1992), p. 182.
8. Quoted with permission: James Marth, M.Div., Jacksonville, Florida (September 1995).
9. M. Scott Peck, M.D., *The Road Less Traveled* (New York: Simon & Schuster, 1978), p. 75.
10. Kathryn Hagen, "Feeling Better With Music," *Arthritis Today* (March/April 1993), vol. 7, no. 2, p. 19.
11. Lyle H. Miller, "Your Personal Stress Reduction Plan," *Executive Female* (May/June 1993), vol. 16, no. 3, p. 29.

Chapter Seven

1. *Consumer Reports on Health* (August 1994), p. 89.

Chapter Eight

1. Leo Buscaglia, Ph.D., *Bus Nine to Paradise* (Thorofare, N.J.: SLACK, Inc., 1986), p. 37.
2. Marjorie Hansen Shaevitz, *Super Woman Syndrome* (New York: Warner, 1984), p. 39.
3. *The Locomotivator* (September/October 1982), p. 37.
4. Judith Sills, Ph.D., "How to Deal With Anger," *Family Circle* (October 11, 1994), p. 10.
5. James Allen Sparks, *Potshots at the Preacher* (Nashville: Abingdon, 1979), p. 79.

Chapter Nine

1. Eugene Kennedy, *The Pain of Being Human* (Garden City, N.J.: Image Books, 1974), p. 38.
2. Leo Buscaglia, Ph.D., *Born for Love* (Thorofare, N.J.: SLACK, Inc., 1992), p. 171.
3. Ray C. Stedman, *Authentic Christianity* (Portland, Ore.: Multnomah Press, 1975), p. 155.
4. Buscaglia, op. cit., p. 175.